THE COSMIC EMBRACE

THE SACRED HEART OF BUDDHA (Tantric *tangka,* Nepal, twentieth century). This intriguing image portrays Buddha at the time of his great awakening, with the added element of a loving couple, locked in cosmic embrace, emerging from his heart. When Buddha was enlightened, he saw "all things in their true nature"; the cosmic lovers revealed here symbolize Buddha's perception of sexual union as the source and center of creation and, on the highest levels of understanding, are a representation of an ideal state of being that is free of duality and opposition. Tantric philosophers believe that if one lacks real understanding of the true dimensions of sex, complete enlightenment is not possible.

THE
COSMIC
EMBRACE

AN ILLUSTRATED GUIDE
TO SACRED SEX

JOHN STEVENS

SHAMBHALA
Boston & London
1999

SHAMBHALA PUBLICATIONS, INC.
Horticultural Hall
300 Massachusetts Avenue
Boston, MA 02115
http://www.shambhala.com

9 8 7 6 5 4 3 2 1

FIRST EDITION
Printed in the United States of America

♾ This edition is printed on acid-free paper that meets the
American National Standards Institute z39.48 Standard.
Distributed in the United States by Random House, Inc.,
and in Canada by Random House of Canada Ltd

LIBRARY OF CONGRESS CATALOGING-IN-PUBLICATION DATA
Stevens, John, 1947–
The cosmic embrace: an illustrated guide to sacred sex/
by John Stevens.—1st ed.
p.   cm.
Includes bibliographical references.
ISBN 1-57062-171-3
1. Sex instruction.   2. Sex—Religious aspects—Tantrism.
I. Title.
HQ64.S74   1999   98-40526
613.9'6—dc21   CIP

CONTENTS

INTRODUCTION

The *Cosmic Embrace: An Illustrated Guide to Sacred Sex* was inspired by a search for the paradise of Shambhala. The enlightened land of Shambhala (or Uttarakuru, as it is sometimes called), is described in the sacred texts of Asia as a lush pleasure garden, warm and inviting, where the words *war* and *hatred* are never heard. Shambhala is peopled with loving couples who are perfectly matched in appearance, spirit, and sexual desire. The couples draw sustenance from a rich nectar of milk and honey, adorn each other with pleasing garlands, delight in music and dance, and sport—in perfect sexual harmony—on beds bedecked with beautiful coverlets and plump cushions. The couples are free from sorrows and ailments, and, most important of all, they never suffer from the pangs of separation. Their boudoirs and other areas of pleasure are decorated with the finest examples of erotic art. This is the same Shambhala witnessed by the eighteenth-century Christian mystic Emanuel Swedenborg, only he called it heaven: "There are angels of both sexes, of a beauty seen nowhere else. Those who were loving couples on earth, are loving couples in heaven; the women have been restored to their virginal beauty, and the men have regained their youthful vitality. Each couple is an embodiment of heavenly love, and their ability to enjoy sexual embrace never ceases."

This book is an exploration of the vision of sacred Shambhala sex—consensual, noncoercive, nonpossessive, mutually fulfilling and beneficial, and totally intimate—as expressed in human culture, past and present, East and West. My primary theme is man and woman as cocreators and cooperative partners—the root of humanity—and I have deliberately avoided the current craze of polarizing cultures, social systems, or religions as either "matriarchal" or "patriarchal." Such distinctions are largely artificial and only serve to incite further antagonism between the sexes.

In keeping with the Tantric tradition that "it is art that most directly reveals the truth," to present my case I have relied more on dramatic visual images (nearly all published here for the first time) than on lengthy quotations, rambling philosophical analysis, or glib popular psychology. Except as noted, all the illustrations and photographs are from my personal collection, and (except as noted) all the quotes that are scattered throughout the book are my own translations and interpretations gleaned from various texts and the oral literature. Because the civilizations of the East are older and more sex positive (in some ways) than those of the West—and because I have spent much of my life in Japan—more of the images and illustrations are taken from Asian traditions. However, the desire to experience liberating sex has always been a universal quest.

The whole creation will . . . appear infinite and holy, whereas it now appears finite and so corrupt. This will come to pass by an improvement of sensual enjoyment. But first the notion that man has a body distinct from his soul is to be expunged. . . . If the doors of perception were cleansed everything would appear to man as it is, Infinite.
—WILLIAM BLAKE, *Marriage of Heaven and Hell*

THE COSMIC EMBRACE

TWO-AS-ONE

Man and Woman as Cocreators of the Universe

> Who does not delight
> In the bliss residing in the
> Union of diamond and lotus?
> Who is not fulfilled there?
>
> —SARAHA, Tantric philosopher

OUR UNIVERSE EXISTS through the interaction of the male and female aspects of creation. The reality of the act of intercourse between a man and a woman, the origin of our life on earth, is a basic component of human consciousness. The two-as-one image conveys that cooperative function in concrete form, and it is found in many different religions and philosophies. The profound two-as-one image is to be contemplated deeply, for as Saraha taught:

> From the union of male and female a pure knowledge
> arises, a knowledge that explains the nature of all things.

FIGURE 1. "All-Good Couple" (*tangka*, Nepal, twentieth century). Hindu and Buddhist Tantric philosophers recognized the central importance of the male-female bond—"Enlightenment is found in the blissful union of man and woman—and they were adamant in displaying that cosmic embrace *yab-yum* (mother-father) on their altars. This particular image is Buddhist: Samantabhadra and his consort Samantabhadrā, the "all-good couple." (In Hinduism the couple would be Shiva/Pārvatī, Krishna/Rādhā, or some other divine pair.) Samantabhadra is the male principle of primordial enlightenment; Samantabhadrā is the female principle of supreme wisdom. The image is concrete—"With kisses and caresses he coaxes his partner into deep embrace; with the jewel [penis] firmly inserted into the lotus [vagina] the couple holds fast to the Buddha vision"—and the metaphysic subtle: the opposing principles of male and female, positive and negative, dynamic energy and receptive energy, individual soul and universal soul, space and time, fire and water, and samsara and nirvana ultimately merge in harmonious balance.

The Buddha couple here are naked, free of artificial adornment, and locked together in an incessant kiss while fused in the ultimate state of creation. Their eyes are open, indicating their eternal awareness of existence as a unified whole, and they function in a realm in which there are no boundaries. Practitioners of Tantra maintain that such an exalted state can be approached only through profound and ardent meditation, but if successful, the body of each partner is transformed from flesh and blood into a vehicle that is golden, adamantine, and perfected.

On a more mundane level, this image represents a common human experience: sexual union with the right partner, at the right time, in the right frame of mind, opens a new window to the world. It also symbolizes what Hindus call a Gandharva marriage: a couple who are intensely attracted to each other ignore all social and religious dictates, abandon all pretense, simply declare their mutual love and then join as one.

FIGURE 2. Mother-Father Buddha of Creation (Falun Temple, northern China, nineteenth century). Tantric thinkers recognized that sex is not always settled and serene; in fact, in order for the world to come into being there must be raging passion. The image here is of a richly adorned "terrific couple" engaged in fierce, unbridled intercourse, and the Chinese characters above read "The Creation of Heaven and Earth." Every living thing owes its existence to the sex drive represented by this wildly copulating Buddha couple. Sex is a tremendous force, and it is not something to be treated lightly or given free reign. Sex can destroy as well as create. Tantric texts warn sternly: "Dealing with sexual energy is more dangerous than walking on the edge of a sword, than clinging to the neck of a raging tiger, than holding a poisonous serpent by the tail."

FIGURE 3. Taoist Couple in the "All-Embracing Posture" (woodcut based on Ming dynasty model, China, c. 1500). Taoist sages taught that "the sexual union of man and woman gives life to all things." To engage in sex—the blending of yin and yang—is to take part in the cosmic act of creation. As we can see here, Taoist partners are truly equal in size, appearance, and expression; there is a delightful sense of sharing in the accomplishment of a sacred task, a sense of active cooperation between the man and woman as they make love in a womblike grotto. This perfectly symmetrical Tao couple are in total accord, rounder and more relaxed than the two Buddha couples of figures 1 and 2. Chan (Zen) Buddhists in China on occasion appropriated this image, since it better represented their interpretation of enlightenment as a circle. Incidentally, the upright sexual posture of this Tao couple is similar to that of the Ain Sakhri figurine (c. 11,000 BC), the oldest representation of human coitus discovered so far.

FIGURE 4. Adam and Eve, by Edward Bawden (ink drawing, illustration for *The World's Greatest Story*, U.S.A., 1978). Portraits have been done in the West of Adam and Eve engaged in intercourse (or even doing it with the beasts of creation), but almost all such portrayals are blatantly sacreligious, if not outright obscene. This portrayal is of an affectionate Adam and Eve, gently making love in the Garden of Eden; it is a sharp contrast to both obscene drawings and religious portraits of Adam and Eve as abject sinners. In certain Christian circles the emphasis has been on the sordidness of Adam and Eve's sexual sin; for centuries many maladjusted and misdirected Christian theologians have held that the Holy Spirit cannot be present during carnal intercourse (there were, and are, plenty of Hindu and Buddhist ascetics who believe the same thing). As we will see later (p. 64), other Christians challenged this view.

The Hebrew and Muslim view of Adam and Eve is more positive. The esoteric schools of both traditions stress the version of Genesis 1:27 ("So God created humankind in his image, in the image of God he created them; simultaneously male and female he created them") rather than the version of Genesis 2:22 ("And the rib that the Lord God had taken from the man, he made into a woman"). A humorous Hasidic tale goes like this:

> The rabbi told his congregation: "God created Adam in his image."
> The congregation replied: "Thanks be to God."
> The rabbi went on, "Then God created Eve, also in his image, but with a difference."
> The congregation responded with enthusiasm, "Thank God for the difference!"

The Muslim vision of Adam and Eve may be summarized this way:

> Adam saw that his partner, Eve, was beautiful; intoxicated by her charm he made love to her, the initial act of intercourse that spawned the great human family. Adam saw that sexual intercourse was good, giving both partners inexpressible joy. He concluded that sex was the most significant act of all those on earth, the greatest of Allah's gifts to humankind.

Jewish Cabalists, Hasidic masters, and Sufi dervishes stressed that the divine presence was most active during sexual union and that "parents are the partners of God," helping to people the universe. In imitation of the holy coupling of Adam and Eve, marriage was incumbent upon all Jews—even though, as some Jewish seers joked, "it is as difficult to correctly match a man and a woman as it was for Moses to part the Red Sea." Tradition held that the Sabbath was the best time for sex. Hasidim were flattered by the criticism of more somber Jews that they "prayed as if they were having intercourse with the female emanation of God." Rabbi Leib Melamed went so far as to state: "One should imagine that a woman stands in front of him during prayer . . . ; one is permitted to have an ejaculation as a result of being aroused by prayer."

FIGURE 5. Alchemical King (Sol) and Queen (Luna) (illustration from *Rosarium Philosophorum,* Europe, 1622). This image occurs in an alchemical text from the mid-seventeenth century, and the accompanying verse has the two partners speaking to each other in turn:

O Luna, enveloped by me
my sweetest one,
you become as fine, strong,
and powerful as I am.
O Sol, brightest of all lights,
You need me as the cock needs the hen.

In Western esoteric systems this royal union of masculine and feminine principles was the key to chemical and psychic knowledge. Part of the Alchemical Oath goes:

The Father (of the One) is of the Sun.
The Mother is of the Moon.
The Wind carried it in its Womb,
And the Earth nursed it.
This is the Source of the world's wonders,
The most perfect power.

The sexual posture (the "missionary position") of the king and queen in this illustration is the one most closely identified with European culture.

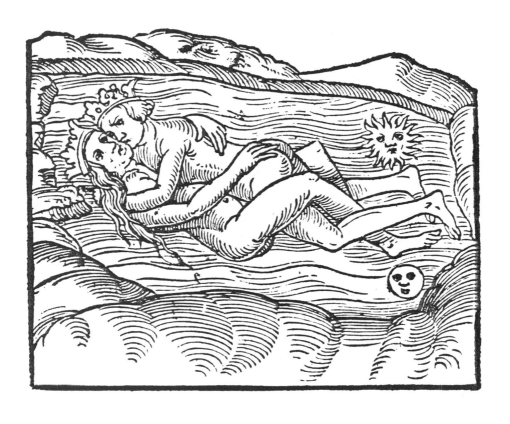

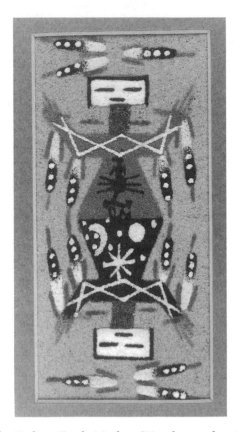

FIGURE 6. Sky Father–Earth Mother (Navaho sand painting, U.S.A., twentieth century). Sky Father envelops the sun, moon, and stars; Earth Mother issues forth the sacred plants: corn, squash, beans, and tobacco. In Native American mythology the union of Sky Father, that which arches over all, and Earth Mother, that which stretches endlessly, sustains the physical world. While the earth is generally associated with the mother principle and the sky with the father principle in world mythology, it is interesting to note that in ancient Egypt the earth is symbolized by the god Geb, who is straddled by the sky goddess Nut.

THE COSMIC YONI AND THE UNIVERSAL LINGAM

T HE TWO-AS-ONE COCREATORS are also worshiped as separate entities, the cosmic yoni (female matrix) and the universal lingam (male creator). These two principles are the signature of life, the marks of being; and symbols of the yoni (vulva) and the lingam (phallus) are found in every culture, sometimes up front and right on the surface, sometimes sublimated and deeply hidden away.

The nurturing yoni symbol predominates in the earliest examples of cave painting and ancient carving uncovered so far. Later on in human history, representations of the lingam become more pronounced. The reasons for this change are not clear, but it may be that, in certain areas, men became more aggressive and thus assertive with their "weapon." Many later paintings depict warriors engaged in battle in a state of sexual excitement. A prime example of this extremely provocative attitude is the gigantic ithyphallic chalk figure cut into the hill above Cerne Abbas in Dorset, England, that bears a huge, threatening club.

Over the centuries the mother principle has ruled some societies, while the father principle has dominated others. We are now rediscovering that for human life to flourish, the cosmic yoni and the universal lingam must be given equal veneration and then conjoined harmoniously.

FIGURE 7. Lajja Gauri (stone carving, India, sixth century, Ajit Mooker-jee Collection). The cosmic yoni is the most ancient of all sexual im-ages—which is most appropriate, since creation is essentially feminine: all fetuses begin as females.

Woman is the creator of the universe.
The universe is her form;
Woman is the foundation of the world,
She is the true form of the body.
Whatever form she takes,
Whether the form of a man or a woman,
Is the superior form.
—Śaktisaṅgama Tantra

Or more succinctly,

Everything you can think of,
Everything you can see,
Is a production of the Goddess.
—JOSEPH CAMPBELL

In India the yoni queen is called Lajja Gauri, "the Shameless God-dess." In this case *shameless* actually means "perfectly modest"; the goddess is free of guilt and inhibition, innocently displaying her womanhood in full glory. The supine Lajja Gauri image is both sexually suggestive—an open invitation to enter—and symbolic of generation, in the pose of giving birth. In Tibet, Lajja Gauri was honored as the Womb Door Sukhasiddhi Dākinī; in the classical world, the goddess was called Baubo, and in the Middle Ages she became known as Sheilah-Na-Gig.

FIGURE 8. Buddhist Nun–Yoni Goddess (stone carving, Kanshōji, Tatebayashi, Japan, eighteenth century). This Shinto-Buddhist goddess is enshrined in a Japanese temple. (Quite similar images adorn churches in Europe, including those of the Vatican, but they are hidden more discretely in corners and at the top of pillars). Pilgrims come to venerate* this statue by touching the sacred yoni and anointing it with red ocher.

In addition to the ultimate exposure posture, a yoni goddess is sometimes depicted performing a magical striptease, raising her skirt and flashing her sex. The Shinto goddess Ame-no-Uzume performed a lascivious dance, exposing her breasts and raising her robe high to reveal her yoni before an assembly of gods, causing such a commotion that the sequestered Sun goddess Amaterasu was lured from her cave, thereby returning light to the world. Medieval European paintings show an empowered woman lifting her skirt and flashing the devil in order to drive him away.

---

*The English word *veneration* is derived from the Latin *veneris* (Venus); one of the ways this Roman goddess was venerated was by the worshipping of her sex organs.

FIGURE 9 (*opposite*). Womb Door Sukhasiddhi Dākinī (Tantric *tangka*, Tibet, nineteenth century; Thomas Kelly: Arnold Lieberman Gallery Collection). The yoni is sacred, a holy of holies, and images such as this graced many temples and homes in Buddhist Tibet.

FIGURE 10 (*above*). The Santeria Mother Goddess Atabey (ceramic, Cuba, twentieth century). The "Respected Mother" opens the door to the inner mysteries of her religion to her devotees, grants the gift of sexual potency, eases childbirth, and heals diseases. Atabey is worshiped with music and song.

FIGURE 11. Blond European Yoni Goddess (pencil sketch, Germany, c. 1930). This modern Western version of the yoni goddess was drawn reverently and in loving detail by an anonymous inmate of a German prison. The yoni—described by Aubrey Beardsley as "a dark, romantic chasm, a cavern in which the wonders of nature abound"—is always a symbol of hope, renewal, and liberation, and should never be spoken ill of or abused.

FIGURE 12. Folk Art Yoni Goddess (house paint on plywood, U.S.A., c. 1970, Gitter Collection). This delightful modern version of the "shameless goddess" is by the contemporary American folk artist Moses Tolliver (1919–). The woman's simple, exuberant, and wide-open display of her sexuality is unaffected and exhilarating.

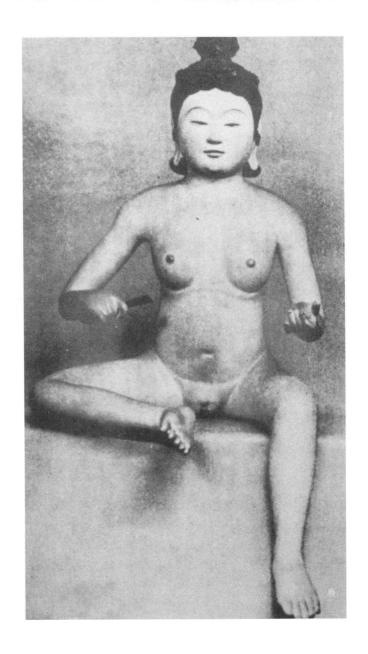

FIGURE 13 (*opposite*). The Yoni Goddess Benzai-ten (wood, Enoshima, Japan, c. 1200). Benzai-ten (Sarasvatī in Sanskrit) is the goddess of art, music, poetry, and physical love. The beautiful "Naked Benzai-ten"— some worshipers literally fall in love with the statue and compose poems and songs in the goddess's honor—enshrined on Enoshima Island near Kamakura is one of the most popular deities in Japan. Benzai-ten represents all the good things of life, and anyone fortunate enough to fully enjoy art, music, poetry, and sex is truly blessed. Benzai-ten is a passionate lover of both gods and men, and she is a special patron of sex workers.

FIGURE 14 (*above*). Yoni Goddess–Sacred Prostitute (ink sketch, France, twentieth century). This goddess is offering her ancestral shrine to a generation of lovers. Prostitution is often terribly squalid and degrading, a base enslavement of a woman's body and mind, but there are occasions when it can be a true calling. The *sobhini* of India and the *hetaerae* of Greece, for example, were among the most beautiful, learned, cultured, wealthy, influential, respected, and liberated women in their respective societies. Not a few women in those (and other) societies became courtesans to escape the drudgery and captivity of an arranged marriage. Holy whores have served at temples and churches throughout recorded history, and it is firmly believed in Asia that Kannon, the goddess of compassion, continually incarnates herself as a courtesan to bring men to salvation through the power of her divine caresses. In the Chinese novel *Jou Pu Tuan* (The Carnal Prayer Mat) there is a description of the courtesan Immortal Maid, a true yoni goddess, Taoist adept, and sacred prostitute:

> Immortal Maid possessed only average looks, but she had been the most popular and wealthiest pleasure girl of the land for thirty years. All of her clients were aristocrats or rich gentry. Immortal Maid was a master of Taoist sex techniques, and she confided to intimate friends, "The delights of life cannot be enjoyed on one's own. Yin must be fitted with yang; when the two principles are in balance, there is real delight. If a woman does not respond to her lover and just lets him pound away, she is nothing more than a mannequin with a hole in it. For mutual fulfillment, yin must actively blend with the yang." After only a few nights with Immortal Maid, her clients became doubly vigorous, with glowing complexions; she herself never seemed to age.

FIGURE 15. Chance Encounter with a Yoni Goddess (ink on paper, Korea, nineteenth century). This fortunate Korean gentleman has been granted a view of a slumbering yoni goddess. An aura of sweet sexuality and natural goodness radiates from the young beauty. Even a chance encounter such as this can be an unforgettable, uplifting experience—another testament to the all-powerful attractive energy of the yoni.

COSMIC EMBRACE

FIGURES 16 *and* 17. Indian Beauty (*opposite*) (stone carving, India, Konarak Temple of the Sun, c. 1200); European Beauty (*above*) (print, France, nineteenth century). Although unlike in composition and created centuries apart in different locales and in distinct cultures—medieval India and nineteenth-century Europe—these two images of earthly angels convey to us all the charm, grace, and irresistible sexual appeal of the feminine form. Here the yoni is shaped like a conch shell, suggesting a cleft to be entered into gently and explored thoroughly; it may also be interpreted as the keyhole of a gate opening to the higher mysteries.

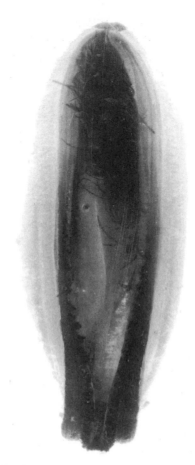

Figure 18. Mollusk Yoni Love Charm (mollusk sealed in Lucite, Japan, twentieth century). The *kteis,* a shell that closely resembles the female love organ, is a cult object the world over. In addition to representing the power of creation and the enticing beauty of the yoni, mollusks rank as one of the most powerful and succulent of aphrodisiacs. (The goddess Aphrodite herself emerged from a shell.) This particular *kteis,* representing a Japanese sea goddess, is used as a miniature shrine and a sex talisman.

FIGURE 19. Yoni Mother with Child (ivory carving, Japan, twentieth century). From the yoni—"the origin of the world"—life issues forth. Childbirth transforms a woman physically, psychologically, and spiritually. The image of motherhood presented here is fertile, rich, and abundantly sexual.

FIGURE 20 (*left*). Naturally Occurring Lingam (lava rock, Hawaii; photograph by Sergio Goes). A lingam is the distinctive sign of masculinity, and its image pops up all over the world, sometimes emerging naturally as a stone formation or as a manmade structure.

FIGURE 21 (*right*). Phallic Skyscraper (Flatiron Building, New York City, 1901)

FIGURE 22. Shinto Lingam (wood, Japan, nineteenth century; photograph by Adam Stevens). This piece of wood was carved into a robust lingam—firm, erect, and noble—and then enshrined as a Shinto deity in a Japanese shrine. Just like a yoni, a lingam is everywhere considered a potent talisman. Yonis are touched but lingams are rubbed for good fortune. When I purchased this lingam in Japan, the two ladies working in the antique shop both gave the head a good rubbing prior to wrapping it up for me to take home.

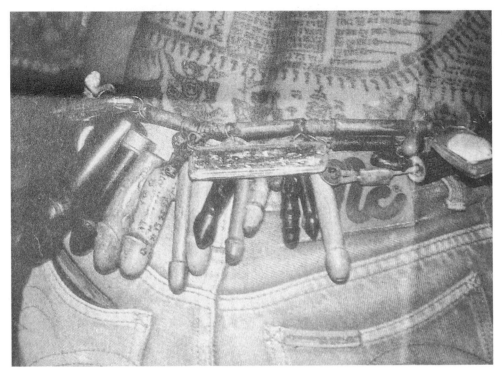

FIGURE 23. Thai Lucky Charm Belt (photo courtesy of Don Ed Hardy). East and West, the lingam is considered a potent charm. Romans often wore a phallic amulet around their necks for good luck and to avert the evil eye, and many men in Thailand wear a belt of miniature lingams around their waists as a talisman.

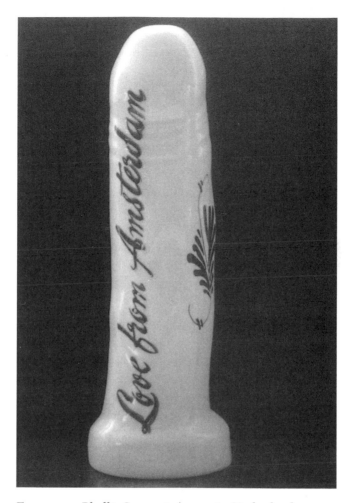

FIGURE 24. Phallic Souvenir (ceramic, Netherlands, twentieth century). Souvenirs such as this are common in Japan, especially from hot spring resorts, but rarer in Western countries. Sex, however, is out in the open in liberal, matter-of-fact Amsterdam, one of the world's foremost sex capitals, and this bold lingam proudly announces that fact.

FIGURE 25. Phallic Snuff Bottle (bone, Tibet, c. 1900; photograph by Adam Stevens). Perhaps fashioned from human bone, this snuff container displays the classic phallic posture: proud, rigid, upright, and thick. This is perhaps the best kind of charm, since it is functional as well as symbolic.

FIGURE 26. Lingam from Bali (wood, Indonesia, twentieth century, Isaac Reawaruw Collection). Male and female figures teem together on the shaft of this lingam, and the wide-open hole at the top suggests a forceful ejaculation, a creamy spurt of creative energy that is capable of bringing countless males and females into existence.

FIGURES 27 *and* 28. Fascinating Phallus from the East (*opposite*) (ivory, Hong Kong, twentieth century); Fascinating Phallus from the West (*above*) (bronze, Vienna, c. 1900; courtesy of the Sex Museum, Amsterdam). A well-formed lingam has the power to fascinate, a word derived from the Latin *fascinum,* a name the Romans used to denote the male sex organ. In certain Japanese hot spring inns, a man-sized lingam is placed in the entrance hall, and women visitors like to be photographed with their arms wrapped affectionately around the pole, not unlike the two images here.

FIGURE 29. Phallic Warrior (koa wood, Hawaii, twentieth century). Unfortunately, the lingam can also be misconstrued as a weapon, and phallic warriors left unpacified can be dangerous. This particular image is less threatening than many others that exist—in most other carvings of this type, the lingam springs out in attack when the shield is lifted—and gives a more balanced sense of bravery combined with ample manhood.

FIGURE 30. Offering to Pan (bas-relief in marble, Pompeii, first century). The principal phallic god in the classical world was Pan/Priapus. Pan was the deity of music, dance, and sex, and he spent his days and nights playing his flute, dancing, and sporting with mountain nymphs. Statues of Pan were erected in fields to ensure an increase of fertility in both crops and human beings. Couples hoping for offspring made offerings to statues of Pan, as seen here, and then engaged in ritual intercourse. (The man hangs a curtain around the statue so that he and his partner can make love undisturbed behind it.)

FIGURE 31. Phallic Christ, by Maerton van Heemskerck (painting, Flanders, 1525; H. Kisters Collection). Many believe that representation and worship of the universal lingam is limited to Asia, but veneration of the phallus is widespread in Europe, albeit more subtly displayed. However, numerous portraits of the phallic Christ in churches show the Savior with a powerful erection. The lingam is the supreme symbol of the life force and eternal rebirth, and it is fitting that it be associated with the notion of resurrection.

At least a dozen churches in Europe claim the Holy Foreskin of Jesus Christ as a relic. Although not to the same extent as in Asia, other phallic stones and shrines dot the European landscape. For example, Saint Foutin was a phallic saint worshiped in France. He was enshrined as a giant lingam in a church at Embrun, in the upper Alps, which was anointed with wine by female parishioners. This wine was collected in a vessel until it turned sour and then used as an aphrodisiac vinegar. Hot cross buns and phallic cookies are still festive foods, and some believe that Saint Nicholas is a baptized Priapus, the phallic god of the Greco-Romans. In the United States, Graceland Cemetery in Chicago is famed for the large number of phallic tombstones on the grounds.

FIGURES 32 *and* 33. Phallic Buddhas (brass, Thailand, twentieth century). Just as there is a phallic Christ, there is a phallic Buddha. Images often have a Buddha holding an ambrosial container, a vase with flowers, a miniature stupa, or a *vajra* on his lap (fig. 32, *opposite*). When some of these images are viewed from above (fig. 33, *above*) or the side, the phallic symbolism is unmistakable. These two particular images portray Gautama Buddha at the time of his enlightenment, another kind of resurrection from the realm of death and despair.

FIGURE 34. Shameless Couple (*above*) (bronze, Southeast Asia, probably Laos, twentieth century). The unabashed display of the yoni and the lingam by this beaming couple is a bold affirmation of the joy, goodness, and rightness of sex. The origin of these little bronzes is likely to be Southeast Asia, but they could be from Africa, South America, or a medieval European church. This uncertainty is indicative of the universal symbolism they reveal.

FIGURE 35. "The Jewel in the Lotus!" (*opposite*) (wood, Ryōsenji, Shizuoka, Japan, nineteenth century). Both the yoni and the lingam are splendid in their own right, but to work magic they have to be united. Worship of the two elemental forces of creation—shown joined here as engorged lingam and enveloping yoni—is the source of all religion, East and West. Ryōsenji, where this image is venerated, is one of several Japanese Buddhist temples and Shinto shrines that are packed

with sexy-Buddha and horny-god icons. At the entrance to one such sex shrine this sign is posted:

Sex is Religion
Sex is Philosophy
Sex is Ethics
Sex is Science
Sex is Human Existence.

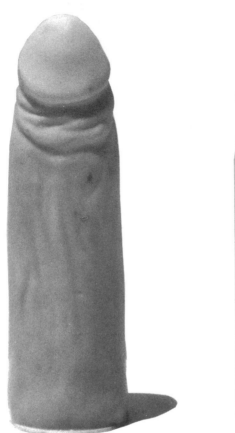

FIGURE 36. American Lingam–Yoni Goddess ("bride and groom" sex toy, molded plastic, U.S.A., c. 1970; photograph by Adam Stevens). Although the treatment of this Americanized pop version of the traditional lingam, complete with a demure yoni-goddess bride concealed within, is lighthearted and the image is mass-produced, this lingam still bears the traditional message: sex is good, pleasant, and creative, best enjoyed with a partner.

FIGURE 37. Natural Lingam-Yoni Rock Formation (Kyūshū, Japan). In nature, too, it is not at all unusual to find a lingam-yoni combination brought into being by the wind and rain. This is a famous natural lingam-yoni rock formation found in Japan. Notice the children in front of the rocks. Japanese parents encourage their children to play near such sites because they are believed to impart good fortune and health to all those nearby.

LOVING COUPLES

T HE IMAGE OF a loving couple in perfect physical and spiritual harmony is a pan-cultural symbol of well-being, peace, and happiness. In this section, loving couples from the East are shown, followed by loving couples from the West, in rough chronological order. The loving couple icon represents another powerful concept that bridges the gap between East and West, past and present.

A Chinese loving couple named Shen Fu and Yen were happily married when Yen fell fatally ill. Shen Fu was only forty years old at the time, and Yen urged her husband to remarry after her death. In reply Shen Fu recited this poem:

> If we part halfway on our journey together
> Rest assured that I will never love another so.
> If you have experienced the Ocean,
> How can a rivulet enthrall you?
> If you have contemplated the Mountain,
> How can you be content with anything less than
>   the summit?

FIGURE 38. *The Immortal Marriage* (watercolor, India, c. 1750; Philadelphia Museum of Art, Stella Kramrisch Collection). Pārvatī fell in love with Shiva and persuaded Kāma, the god of love, to shoot a flower arrow at the fierce ascetic's heart in order to rouse him from his deep meditation. Shiva emerged from his trance, and the sight of Pārvatī, all ravishing beauty and radiance, inflamed his passions, but he resisted the enticing charms of the lovely goddess until she proved herself equal in ascetic determination— Pārvatī fasted as severely as Shiva and imitated his meditation, sitting next to a blazing fire and then immersing herself in an icy stream. Finally smitten, Shiva wed Pārvatī. (Pārvatī's mother initially opposed the match because she considered Shiva no more than a penniless vagabond.) In this touching portrayal, Shiva—still clad in the garb of a wandering ascetic, his worldly possessions contained in a sack hanging from a tree branch—gently caresses his beloved partner Pārvatī, who has fallen asleep peacefully in his lap. The scene conveys a sense of pure connubial bliss in a natural and serene setting.

Just as in real life, things did not always go so smoothly between the divine pair. Shiva and Pārvatī had some mighty quarrels—one occurred when he was droning on about the meaning of the scriptures and she fell asleep—but they always managed to reconcile, sometimes locked in intense intercourse for a thousand years. According to one tradition, the god Brahma surreptitiously created discord between Shiva and Pārvatī in order to increase their sexual ardor. Like many couples, following each quarrel Shiva and Pārvatī would make up with an increased passion, eventually building to such a crescendo that any issue born of that union between these two immortals would surely be a world savior.

FIGURE 39. Izanagi and Izanami (painting on silk, Japan, c. 1930). Izanagi ("He Who Invites") and Izanami ("She Who Invites"), the original loving couple of Japan, realized that each had something the other needed for fulfillment, but they were not sure how to go about getting it. The two deities then noticed a pair of mandarin ducks joined together, bobbing their tails. This gave Izanami and Izanagi the general idea, which they then put into practice. The sexual congress of these two deities produced the land and every living thing. Paintings such as this often grace the opening page of Japanese pillow books, guides to lovemaking for newly married couples, and serve as a sanction and inspiration.

FIGURE 40. Heavenly Loving Couples (stone carvings, India, Konarak Temple of the Sun, c. 1200). Lovers on earth should emulate the lovers in heaven. An inscription on one of the erotic temples of Khajuraho says: "May the laughter of Shiva while he sports with his consort Pārvatī inspire you." Early Western visitors to India were shocked by the sight of temples covered with beaming loving couples bound together like creepers, but as Joseph Campbell perceptively remarked, "Couples celebrating love are exactly what should be on a religious edifice." And such images appear on Christian churches in Europe far more than most people realize (see Weir and Jerman's *Images of Lust* in the bibliography).

LOVING COUPLES | 51 |

FIGURE 41 (*opposite*). Royal Lovers (wood, Nepal, eighteenth century). The third eyes of both the king and queen have opened, enabling them to perceive the great wisdom that permeates the sexual embrace. Here is a description of two royal lovers from a Buddhist text:

> Her hair is dark, her eyes lotus blue; her voice is clear, her complexion golden; her breasts are heavy, her waist is slender, and her hips full; a fragrance of sandalwood wafts from her body, and when she smiles, heavenly music plays. His hair is black and curly, his eyes large and dark; his skin is cool and smooth, his body well built and agile; his voice is irresistible and his smile dazzling.

FIGURE 42 (*following pages*). Shāh Jahān and Mumtāz Mahal, One of History's Preeminent Loving Couples (miniature paintings, India, twentieth century). Although Shāh Jahān (d. 1666) had access to just about any woman in his empire, Mumtāz Mahal (d. 1631) was his favorite consort by far and she was also his most trusted advisor. These splendid miniature paintings capture the intense affection between the royal lovers, and we can sense their eternal bond even though they are not in physical contact. Lady Mumtāz died tragically in her thirties while giving birth to the couple's fourteenth child. Jahān never recovered from the loss of his heart mate, and as a monument to his undying love for Mumtāz he had a mausoleum constructed for her. That edifice, the Taj Mahal, may be the most beautiful building in existence.

FIGURE 43. *Dōso-jin* Statue (stone, Japan, nineteenth century). *Dōso-jin* loving couples are found all over Japan at crossroads, in rice fields, on the grounds of temples and shrines, and on family altars. The loving couple here are dressed as monk and nun—in Japanese both *holy* and *sexual* are connoted by one word, *sei*. Such dōso-jin statues were often placed at village boundaries to serve as talismans against external evil forces. The statues declare to the outside world that the men and women within the protected area are united as one and not easily attacked. *Dōso-jin* come in a variety of forms: Izanagi-Izanami couples, prince and princess couples, monk and nun couples, whispering couples, sake-drinking couples, dancing couples, chubby couples, arm-in-arm couples, kissing couples, and lovemaking couples. The presence of loving couples everywhere is a constant reminder of the blessings of sex for humankind.

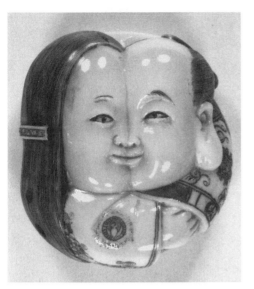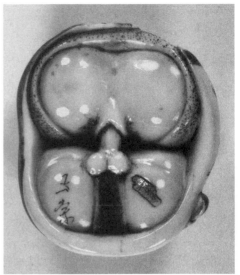

FIGURE 44. Fused Loving Couple (ivory *netsuke,* Japan, twentieth century). The coupling here is so complete, front and back, that the pair merge together perfectly, just made for each other. It is often observed that longtime, happily married couples begin to look more like twins than husband and wife.

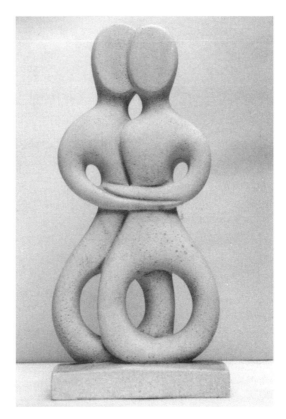

FIGURE 45 (*opposite*). Zen Loving Couple (sumi ink, Japan, nineteenth century; private collection). The inscription on this ink drawing by Tesshū Yamaoka (1836–1888) reads, "You will live to be one hundred, I'll live to be ninety-nine, as our hair turns white together." This old couple may not have much physical contact, but they have grown as close as can be over the years and are truly intimate.

FIGURE 46 (*above*). Cycladic Loving Couple (museum reproduction). The original marble image on which this reproduction is based dates back to the third millennium BC. This simple carving radiates a timeless sense of shared intimacy.

FIGURE 47. *Mars and Venus,* by Agostino Carracci (print, from *The Loves of the Gods,* Italy, c. 1602). The ancient myth of Mars (god of war) and Venus (goddess of love) has been appropriated by contemporary American pop psychologists to reaffirm old stereotypes, but in this print Venus clearly has the upper hand. She has disarmed Mars completely and is actively pacifying the god of war with the full force of her feminine charms. Venus seems to be saying to Mars: "There are wars because people have forgotten that sex is sacred; wanton sex and a life without love lead to chaos and death. Stay here away from the battlefield and let me make love to you." Good sex will, as Venus asserts, temper a person's violent tendencies, and that is not what some unfortunate competitive types want. In the arena of big-time sports, misguided coaches often try to deny their players access to sex before an important game in the belief that such deprivation makes a human being meaner and more aggressive, better able to destroy—not merely defeat—an opponent. On the other hand, the English National Ballet recently urged its dancers to have sex before a show to inspire them to make their performances more passionate.

FIGURE 48. Classical Loving Couple (bronze, Corinth, c. 325 BC; gift of Fiske Warren and W. P. Warren, courtesy Museum of Fine Arts, Boston). This charming portrayal of an obviously experienced human couple making love, with the god Eros hovering above holding a garland for the couple, is lush and sensual. All over the world, loving couples have adorned everyday utensils such as this mirror cover; people enjoy being reminded of the delights and blessings of sex.

FIGURE 49. Loving Couple Forever (alabaster sarcophagus lid, Etruscan, c. 330–300 BC; gift of Mrs. Gardner Brewer, courtesy Museum of Fine Arts, Boston). An extremely touching rendition of a classical loving couple, embracing naked in bed while gazing tenderly into each other's eyes. This is the effigy the couple wished to have carved on the cover of their joint tomb, where they would lie together, united always.

Figure 50. *The Nuptials of God,* by Eric Gill (engraving, Britain, 1922; Victoria and Albert Museum, London). Despite official condemnation, there has been a persistent and widespread belief in the West that Mary Magdalen and Jesus Christ were lovers who married. In the Gospel of Philip, written in the second half of the third century and part of the Nag Hammadi find, Mary Magdalen is described as Christ's "consort," whom "He loved more than all the disciples, frequently showering her with kisses." Martin Luther, in his *Table Talks* published in 1532, expressed the belief that Christ had sex with Mary Magdalene and other women in order to be fully human. In modern times the contention that Christ had a soul bride in Mary Magdalen has surfaced in books such as *The Last Temptation of Christ* by Nikos Kazantzakis (which was also made into a controversial film). It is unfortunate that orthodox Christianity could not allow for a savior who was like Shiva: great spiritual ascetic as well as magnificent lover of the flesh.

However, there has always been a strong undercurrent of sacred sexuality in the Christian world. In the early days of the church, certain sects such as the Nicolaites held that the best way to salvation was through ecstatic intercourse between the sexes—that was the real communion. The Adamites celebrated mass in the nude, and then all members participated in a sexual love feast. In their secret diaries, some Christian women wrote of their love affairs with the Lord, sensuous encounters that left them "spent with fatigue after receiving divine embraces" and "no longer a virgin." Nearly every cathedral in Europe has at least one statue of a female saint in orgasmic ecstasy, the most famous being the image of Saint Teresa of Ávila in the church of Santa Maria della Vittoria in Rome. In modern times the Catholic artist Eric Gill (1882–1940) created some of the most erotic and beautiful Christian images ever produced.

FIGURE 51. Bishop and Deaconess (?) Blessing the Nuptial Bed of a Naked Christian Couple (woodcut, Germany, c. 1450). In medieval Roman Catholic Europe it was the custom for a bishop to bless the bed of a newly married couple, a sanctification of their sexual union. In woodcuts depicting this ceremony, the bishop is usually accompanied by a woman who gestures in an attitude of prayer and blessing, indicating a sacerdotal function. The couple in this particular woodcut gaze at each other longingly, eager to consummate their marriage in a blessed state of bliss.

FIGURE 52. African Loving Couple (wood, Tanzania, twentieth century; photograph by Adam Stevens). The two-as-one icon is a central theme in African art, representing mythical progenitors, ancestral matriarchs and patriarchs, or simply a happily married local couple.

FIGURE 53. Maori Tattooed Loving Couple (wood, New Zealand, nineteenth century). These two lovers, Hinemoa and Tutanekai, were from feuding clans but they managed to overcome all obstacles and unite. Their union led to a peace pact between the two clans. Such images were carved on doorways as protective talismans and served as a constant reminder of the need for love and harmony in life.

FIGURE 54. Mexican Loving Couple (by contemporary folk artist Josefina Aguilar, clay, Mexico, c. 1985; photograph by Adam Stevens). Though not explicit, this figurine nonetheless depicts a highly erotic expression of passionate lovers.

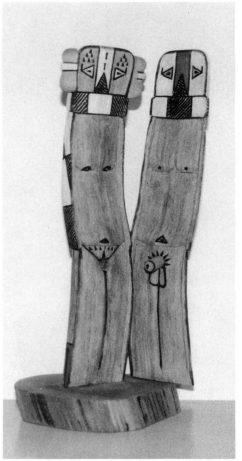

FIGURE 55. Mr. and Mrs. Kokopelli (wood, Hopi tribe, twentieth century). Kokopelli is a flute-playing fertility god honored by Native American tribes in the Southwest. His wife is Kokopelli-mana. In this captivating wooden carving the couple fits together comfortably (left), but the pair may also be separated (right)—the doll can thus serve as a two-as-one icon or as individual cosmic yoni–universal lingam symbols.

FIGURE 56. Kitsch Loving Couple (ceramic, U.S.A., c. 1950s; photograph by Adam Stevens). The irresistible attraction to the opposite sex (Hindu sex manuals say that "lovers will brave darkness, storms, snakes, and demons to keep a tryst") exists even in inanimate objects. The dealer who originally owned these two pieces initially acquired only the male cup. At a large antiques fair he had the cup on display when an unknown woman dealer suddenly appeared carrying the missing female partner. The woman announced, "These two belong together," handed the female cup to the dealer, and walked away.

Figure 57. Folk Art Loving Couple, by Jimmie Lee Sudduth (1910–) (earth pigments, vegetable dyes, and house paint on plywood, U.S.A., c. 1985; Gitter Collection). A pose similar to the one displayed by this couple from the deep South of the United States—man and woman with hands on each other's genitals—is sometimes seen in Japanese *dōso-jin* statues. Loving couples everywhere have much in common. (Folk artists often use both sides of a board when they paint; in this case, one side was hung first, so this side became the back, hence the wire.)

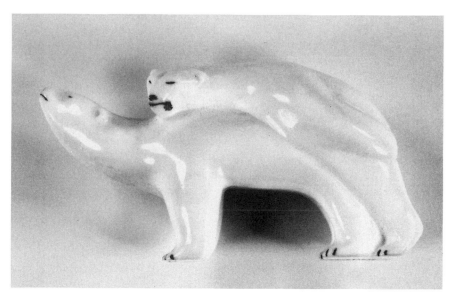

FIGURE 58. Loving Couple Polar Bears (ivory, Inuit art, U.S.A., twentieth century). The joys of sex are not limited to human beings, as demonstrated here by this blissed-out animal couple. There is an interesting legend regarding the selection of Darius the Great (r. 522–486 BC) as king of Persia. When the previous king died without designating a successor, the principal chiefs agreed to ride out to a certain hill at daybreak the following morning, and the owner of the first horse to neigh in greeting to the rising sun would be declared the new ruler. That night Darius had his horse and a young mare in heat taken secretly to that hill and allowed to mate. The horse was brought back to Darius, which he then mounted and rode off to the hill, timing it so that they would reach the top at sunrise. As soon as Darius's horse got to the top, it began to neigh in anticipation, and Darius was proclaimed king.

FIGURE 59. Loving Couple Parsnip Roots (U.S.A., c. 1920). If you garden long enough, you will be sure to turn up yoni-lingam vegetables
and fruit, and sooner or later you will encounter some form of plant
life making love with itself.

EROTIC ART

E VERY CULTURE has produced erotic art—indeed, many artists have declared the entire world one vast work of erotic art. Art that emerges from the erotic sentiment—intense, refined, and exhilarating—is always worth viewing and contemplating. However, in many societies there are antisex crusaders who do not recognize erotic art as an essential element of the common human heritage and therefore attempt to suppress it under the pretense of religious morality or acceptable social standards. After a long and difficult struggle it is much easier now in the West to openly display and appreciate erotic art. For decades the British Museum, possessor of perhaps the world's largest collection of erotica, kept that material under strict lock and key. In recent years, however, the museum has published a wonderful little book, *Erotica,* containing color photographs of some of the best pieces in their collection, and we look forward to the day when that collection has its own wing for permanent display. Ironically, in much of the Middle East and Asia, the source of many erotic masterpieces, the freedom to display such art has ceased to exist, so the struggle continues.

In many cultures, erotic art was perceived as the ultimate goodluck charm. As a manifestation of irrepressible creative energy, erotic art was imbued with the magic power to ward off evil, to overwhelm the forces of darkness and despair, and to protect against natural disasters. Erotic talismans are worn on one's person, sewn into clothes, drawn on a child's bed, set near doorways, placed in chests and on shelves, tucked into books, and carried into battle.

Although there is a distinct difference between erotic art and pornography, many claim to have trouble distinguishing between the two. However, I have examined thousands of pieces of sex-related material over the years, and I have rarely hesitated in deciding which were inspiring erotic art and which were disgusting, obscene trash. Good erotic art cherishes, celebrates, and elevates sex; pornography cheapens, degrades, and negates it. Erotic art presents the sexual experience in a bright, positive, and sympathetic manner; pornography relishes violence, violation, and perversion. In the Far East, erotic art is called *shunga*, "spring pictures." The experience of real love is often compared to basking in an eternal spring, and savoring erotic art is a way to share in that bliss.

Viewing erotic art can have a mesmerizing impact. In both East and West there are many tales of artists falling in love with their creations (in some myths, the images come to life in response to that passion) or of worshipers whose devotion is so extreme that they actually make love to religious icons. A photographer once confided that photographing the erotic images of the temples at Khajuraho in India gave him frightful erections and that one statue in particular entranced him so much that he spent his nights making love to it in his dreams.

A brief introduction to the principal forms of world erotic art follows, with representative illustrations for each tradition.

FIGURE 60 (*previous page*). A Chinese Gentleman with His Wives and Concubines (watercolor, China, nineteenth century). Detailed sex manuals were likely first produced in China. There were at least eight texts describing the art of the bedchamber circulating in China well before the Christian era. Several of them are attributed to the mythical Yellow Emperor, who flourished five thousand years ago. The basic principle of traditional Chinese philosophy was "The interaction of the female essence [yin] with the male essence [yang] is the Way of Life (Tao)." Enjoyable and productive sexual intercourse—"the coiling of the dragon and the tiger"—was essential for the well-being both of individuals and of society as a whole. Good sex could cure mental and physical ills, assure success in business, and protect against misfortune. "Master the Art of the Bedchamber and your years will be prolonged; you will grow old vigorously, gracefully, and peacefully."

As can be seen in this illustration, sex among the Chinese upper classes was a group affair. The Yellow Emperor was said to have obtained immortality after having sex with twelve hundred women, and the Queen of the West retained her youthful beauty by having intercourse with a steady succession of teenage boys. A Chinese gentleman typically had several wives and a number of concubines whom he was duty-bound to satisfy. Here the master of a wealthy Chinese household dallies with one of his wives, assisted by two other female members of the family. One of the ladies offers him a restorative cup of tea. In Chinese erotic art, interested onlookers are often present; in this painting the master's performance inspires his son to embrace a nearby maid, who willingly reciprocates. Chinese erotic art typically possesses this kind of dreamy aura, suggesting that sex exists on a different plane.

FIGURE 61. Happy Chinese Lovers (watercolor, China, nineteenth century). Here in a more down-to-earth scene, an ordinary couple enjoys "clouds and rain," the Chinese term for sexual intercourse.* This happy, naked pair do not need a lot of props and attendants in order to delight in each other and harmonize their lovemaking with nature. The four characters across the top read, from right to left: "Wind, Flowers, Snow, Moon," representing the glorious gifts Mother Nature gives to lovers.

---

*The origin of the term comes from this legend: In a dream, a Chinese prince beheld a woman of surpassing beauty. She came to him and they made love the entire night. As she got ready to depart in the morning, the prince asked her who she was. Her reply: "I am she who brings the clouds in the morning; I am she who calls up the rain at night."

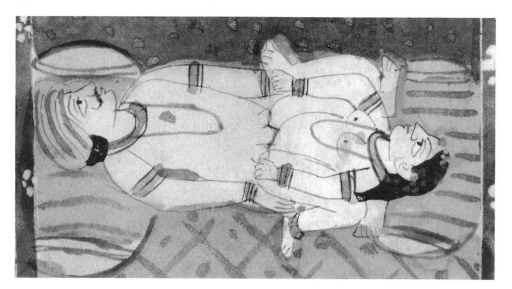

FIGURES 62 *and* 63. Indian Lovers Contemplating Each Other (*opposite*) (watercolor, nineteenth century); Tantric Sex (*above*) (watercolor, India, nineteenth century). India is as famed as China for its long and glorious tradition of erotic art and literature—the *Kama Sutra* is the most famous sex manual in the world—but the culture has a split personality regarding sex: "Two things alone are of real value in this world: the peace of monastic renunciation or the delight of being in a lover's arms." India has been, simultaneously, the most erotic and the most ascetic of world cultures. Vātsyāyana, the compiler of the *Kama Sutra*, is reputed to have been a celibate monk. In Taoist China sex was always viewed as a lifelong pursuit, but orthodox Hindus considered sex a valid but temporary pleasure—nirvana was best obtained by eventually extinguishing all passion.

Thus, in classical Indian erotic art there is generally a certain reserve and detachment present. Couples are often shown motionless, gazing quietly into each other's eyes (fig. 62), or in a paired yoga posture serenely circulating their respective sexual energy (fig. 63). Individual sexual union is always linked to cosmic consciousness: "Locked in embrace with a lover, totally dissolved in the feeling of oneness, with no sense of external and internal; so is the experience when the mind is united with Brahman."

FIGURES 64 *and* 65. Japanese Lovers (*above*) (woodblock print, Japan, nineteenth century); Another Pair of Passionate Japanese Lovers (*opposite*) (painting on silk, Japan, twentieth century). Japan is the third great erotic empire of the senses. In terms of output, it is likely that more erotic art—both fine and folk—was produced in Japan over the centuries than in any other land. In sharp contrast to the reserved and stately depiction of sexual intercourse in India and China, the exuberance of the lovers in Japanese *shunga* is unequivocal. Couples are shown with their huge, dripping-wet love organs joined in total abandon;

men and women are often presented in the throes of orgasmic bliss, something almost never seen in Chinese and Indian erotic art. The Japanese shared the belief of the Chinese that sex was good for people—the inscription on figure 64 alludes to sex as being the best of all medicines—but they were hardly afraid to ejaculate. In figure 64 the crumpled tissues strewn about indicate that this is the couple's second or third round of the night, and in figure 65 love juice spills over from the lady's yoni.

FIGURE 66 (*above*). Nepalese Erotic Art (bronze, based on a carving at the Char Narain Temple, Nepal, twentieth century). The temples of Nepal rival those of India in terms of quantity and quality of the erotic art displayed on the columns and eaves. The Nepalese approach the subject of sex with more humor and less reserve, as can be seen here in this statue of two half-human–half-beast figures madly going at it. The little figure to the right appears to be both venerating and smiling at the act.

FIGURE 67 (*opposite*). Tibetan Loving Couple, by Romio Shrestha (painting, Nepal, twentieth century). Many painted and sculpted masterpieces of the *yab-yum* (mother-father) image were created in Tibet, but for some reason the Tibetans produced very little secular erotic art. This is a rare modern example of a human Tibetan loving couple, and it was commissioned for a medical text, not a sex manual. Perhaps the Tibetans were too busy having sex and had no time (or need) to depict it in art. While the Tibetans had a thoroughly Buddhist culture, their sexual mores were among the most relaxed and permissive in any nation. Just about every kind of marriage arrangement—monogamous, polygy-

nous, polyandrous, group—was acceptable, and many monks and nuns had a sexual consort. There were in fact several famed sex saints in Tibet, the most beloved being the sixth Dalai Lama. Here are three of his love poems:

> I long for the landlord's daughter,
> A perfect ripe peach
> Pining away
> On the highest branches.

> Using astrology
> I can easily measure the stars;
> Yet intimate as I am with her soft body,
> I cannot fathom the depth of her love.

> I seek counsel from a wise lama
> To escape from my predicament;
> But my mind remains captivated
> By my sweetheart.

FIGURES 68 *and* 69. Thai Folding Book (*opposite*) (watercolor, Thailand, c. 1930); Thai Erotic Vignette (*above*) (watercolor, Thailand, c. 1930). Thailand is another Buddhist land with tolerant, easygoing sexual mores. Unlike in Tibet, Thai Buddhist monks are expected to be strictly celibate, but laypeople (and foreign visitors) have a lot of sexual freedom. Thai erotic art is characterized by hidden scenes—a lighthearted portrayal of a couple in sexual embrace tucked away in a corner—incorporated into a larger framework (fig. 68). This is true even of Thai temple mural painting—one is sure to find an erotic vignette concealed somewhere on the temple wall. And there is usually a Peeping Tom or Peeping Mary spying on the lovers (fig. 69).

FIGURE 70. Balinese Lovers (ink on treated paper, Indonesia, nineteenth century; Royal Institute of Linguistics and Anthropology, Netherlands). Bali is a sexual paradise, and erotic art is found everywhere; erotic souvenirs are now a mainstay of the tourist industry. As in Thailand, Balinese eroticism is relaxed and natural, and sex is pretty much indulged in for the fun of it rather than for profound philosophical or medical reasons as in China or India.

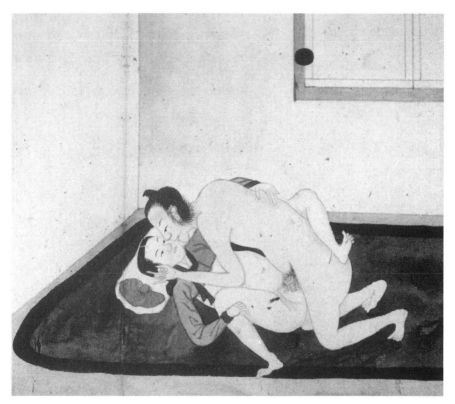

FIGURE 71. Korean Lovers (watercolor, Korea, nineteenth century). Confucian puritanical conservatism had a deleterious effect on erotic art in Korea. The Confucian Li dynasty ruthlessly suppressed any public display of erotic art (although, as in all lands, country folk continued to worship fertility gods). This painting is a very rare example of Korean erotic art. The tenderness shown by the male partner to his female lover is especially touching.

FIGURE 72. Muslim Lovers (painting on ivory, India, twentieth century). Islam is perhaps the most sex positive of all the world religions. Muhammad had nine wives, and we know far more about his sex life than about any other great religious figure's. According to oral tradition he is reported to have declared, "In this world, I love women and perfume most," and "Allah made intercourse so pleasurable and attractive that it is imperative to enjoy sex fully with every nerve and every muscle." Muhammad made it grounds for divorce if a husband failed to meet the sexual needs of his wife at least once a week. Muhammad himself made love to his wives every chance he could, and he massaged his penis every morning with distilled henna water to keep it in good shape. Once, however, Muhammad's sex drive waned and he complained to the angel Gabriel. Gabriel gave the Prophet this sound advice: "Eat a lot of *herisa* [mutton and wheat flour] and truffles and regularly dine on eggs, seafood, lentils, bull testicles, chicken, carrots, almonds, dates, and asparagus. And lose a few pounds. A big belly impedes you sexually." There are a number of Islamic sex manuals—*The Perfumed Garden* is second only to the *Kama Sutra* in world popularity—but owing to the restriction on representing the human form in Islam, explicit erotic art is comparatively rare, found mostly in Persia or Turkey. (Jewish erotic art is even rarer, perhaps nonexistent—I have yet to encounter a truly explicit example). Here a Muslim gentleman offers a cup of wine to his partner as they prepare for lovemaking.

FIGURE 73. Mochica Erotic Pot (clay reproduction, Peru, original c. 600). Pre-Columbian erotic art, mostly in earthenware, is noted for its humorous bawdiness. Many drinking vessels, for example, required the drinker to receive the liquid through a penis-shaped spout or from a vulvalike hole.

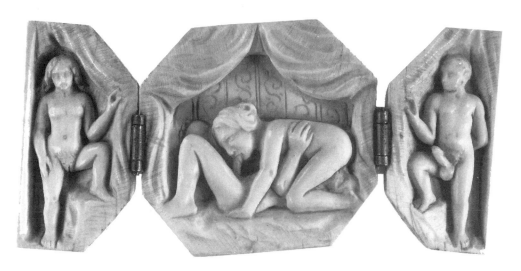

FIGURE 74. Erotic European Triptych (ivory locket, France, nineteenth century). This triptych has all the elements of classical European erotic art. Both the attendants on the side panels are athletically built, with well-proportioned sex organs, and they appear confident and self-assured of their sexuality. None of the participants has adornment of any kind—none of the fancy clothes, splendid coiffures, elaborate jewelry, and heavy makeup seen in Asian erotica. In the classical world of Western erotica, an unclad, healthy human body is so alluring that it requires no embellishment.

FIGURE 75. Bucolic European Lovers (painted ivory pill box, France, nineteenth century). The lady in this painting has a fuller, more Rubenesque figure than the woman in the previous example, and the painting has a softer, more romantic focus typical of eighteenth- and nineteenth-century European art.

FIGURE 76. Offering to Pan (print, France, nineteenth century). Here a young girl garlands a statue of Pan while rubbing her body against the sex organ of the image. This lithograph is by Jean Francois Millet (1814–1875), the famous French artist who painted *The Angelus,* one of the most profoundly moving religious works of art ever created. Most of the great artists of the East and the West produced erotic art— Picasso's most erotic work was done when he was eighty-seven, and he was drawing erotic subjects into his nineties.

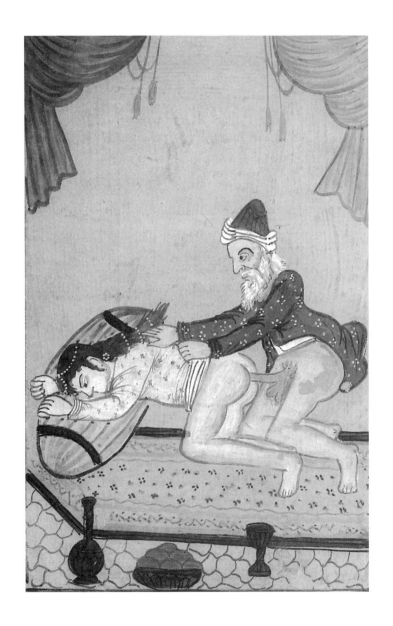

FIGURES 77, 78, *and* 79. Older Man with Younger Woman (*opposite*) (water-color on paper, Persia, nineteenth century); Young Man with Older Woman, by Fernand Couders (*above*) (print, France, 1926); Older Couple Enjoying Each Other (*following page*) (painting on silk, China, Ming dynasty; from *Dreams of Spring,* courtesy the Pepin Press, Amsterdam). An older man making love to a younger woman (fig. 77) is a common theme in erotic art and literature, as are depictions of a young man being initiated into the arts of love by a more experienced woman (fig. 78), but there are not enough examples of older couples still delighting in each other's loving company (fig. 79).

FIGURE 80. "I'll Show You Mine If You Show Me Yours" (print by Martin Van Maele, France, c. 1907). Sex is generally reckoned as serious business, and humor in erotic art is not as prominent as perhaps it should be, but this whimsical scene sketched circa 1907 captures well a common human experience.

FIGURE 81. Initiation in Love (watercolor, France, c. 1940; courtesy Erotic Print Society). Heretofore erotic art was largely produced by men, but in the twentieth century a number of women have created highly sensual art. This delectable painting was done by the French artist Suzanne Ballivet (n.d.) to illustrate the anonymously written book *Initiation Amoureuse* (Initiation in Love), privately published in 1943.

FIGURE 82. The Joy of Sex (bronze, New Zealand, 1973; John and Trish Gribben Collection, photo by Tonia Matthews). Here is an intriguing piece of contemporary erotic sculpture by Paul Beadle (1917–1993) showing a shepherd and his partner in wild abandon. Erotic art and its positive sexual imagery needs to be brought right into the open, without cant or pretention.

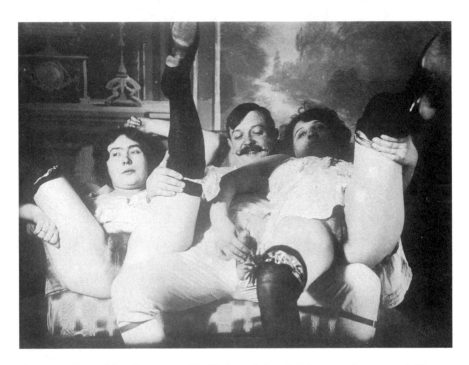

FIGURES 83 *and* 84. European Frollickers (*above*) (nineteenth century); Young Chinese Loving Couple (*opposite*) (nineteenth century). As soon as photography was developed in the nineteenth century, anonymous erotic pictures began to circulate, and there has been a love affair between the camera and

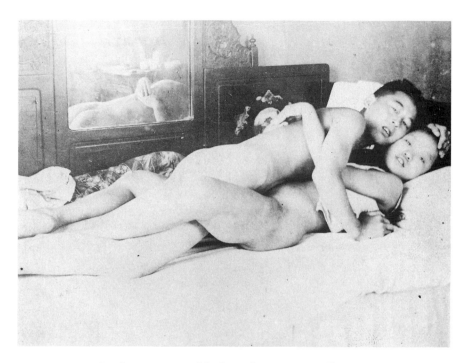

sex ever since. In this amusing old photo from Europe (fig. 83), the two ladies assume the classic yoni-goddess open-invitation posture, while one of them primes the pleased gentleman's pump. In figure 84, a young Chinese couple poses for the camera.

FIGURE 85. "To Freddie with All My Love, Genda, 2-11-13" (photographer unknown). A nude photograph of one's lover is a kind of good-luck charm as well as a pleasant reminder of past and future joys.

FIGURE 86. Chinese Erotic Folk Art (painting on glass, China, nineteenth century). Erotic folk art tends to be more earthy and unabashed than "fine" art by professionals. Judging from the little swirls on the scroll in the background, the folk artist who did this painting on glass was illiterate and untrained, but nonetheless the work has a pleasing effect.

FIGURE 87. Folk Art Figurine of Adam and Eve (glass, Italy, twentieth century).
Erotic folk art also displays a lot of wry humor. Here, sexy Eve and virile Adam
are caught red-handed, with their pants down (so to speak) and expressions on
their faces of "Oh, boy! What have we gotten into?" The joined hands of the
pair further suggests that Adam and Eve were true partners in their mischief
and that Eve should not be made to bear all the blame for their "sin."

FIGURE 88. Mexican Erotic Folk Art (clay, Mexico, twentieth century; photograph by Ric Noyle). Mexican folk artists love to create erotic pieces; here if you lift up the chicken you will find more than a few eggs in the nest.

FIGURE 89. Peekaboo Erotic Folk Art (Hakata ceramic, Japan, twentieth century). "Peekaboo" folk art is popular the world over. In this example from Japan, the stern Zen patriarch Daruma is actually a front for passionate sex—suggesting that we cannot always judge a book by its cover.

FIGURE 90. Erotic Peekaboo Frogs (iron, origin unknown, twentieth century). These two peekaboo frogs are amusing examples of anthropomorphic erotic art. It is impossible to distinguish the gender from above, but turn them over and there is no mistaking which sex is which. Sexy frogs appear worldwide in folk erotica. In the United States I was told these frogs likely came from Japan; in Japan I was informed that they were probably produced in the United States. It doesn't matter, because the message is loud and clear.

FIGURE 91. Krishna the Hero and Krishna the Lover (black paint on dried palm leaf, India [Orissa], twentieth century). Here is a more complex form of peeka-boo folk art from India. On the surface we find depictions of miraculous scenes

from Krishna's heroic life (*opposite*); flip the top half of each circle over (*above*) and we can see Krishna exploring the mysteries of sex with his love partner Rādhā.

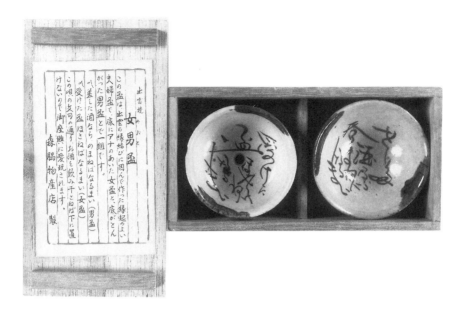

FIGURE 92. Female and Male Sake Cups (ceramic, Japan, twentieth century). Folk art naturally conveys a lot of folk wisdom, as seen here with these sake cups. As the inscription on the box lid explains: "The male cup (right) has a pointed bottom, and the female cup (left) has a hole in its center. Neither cup can function on its own—the sake will leak from the hole in the center of the female cup and spill over the side of the wobbly male cup—but put them together, with the male point in the female hole, and the cups form a stable container." The moral is clear: in order for society to function well, men and women have to join forces and complement each other.

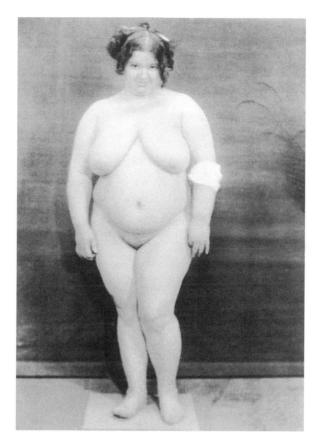

FIGURE 93. American Willendorf (U.S.A., Raphael Studio, 1928; New Orleans Museum of Art, museum purchase, Robert Gordy Fund). Representation of the nude female form appears to be the oldest type of human-crafted art. Examples of fleshy, Earth Mother nudes date back as far as 300,000 BC (the Acheulian Goddess), and the Willendorf Venus (30,000 BC) is now one of the most famous works of art in the world. This artistic "American Willendorf" is a proud representative of the primordial mother goddess tradition.

FIGURES 94 *and* 95. European Nude (*above*) (photographer unknown); Indian Nude on Display (*opposite*) (watercolor on paper, India, twentieth century). European nudes are typically totally naked: "The body itself is perfect and complete," while nudes from Southeast Asia are almost always richly adorned with jewelry and other accessories: "Beauty needs to be enhanced to reach its pinnacle."

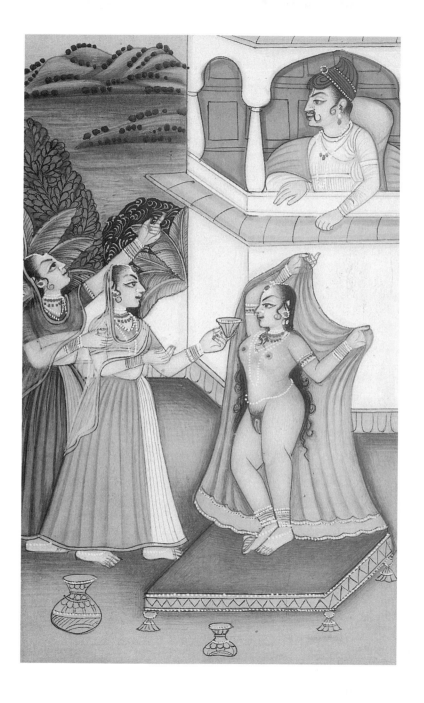

FIGURES 96 *and* 97. Chinese Doctor's Lady (*above*) (ivory, China, twentieth century); European-Style Doctor's Lady (*opposite*) (ivory, Japan, twentieth century). Naked "doctors' ladies" were originally created in China to allow aristocratic women to point to the place on the doll where they were ailing on their own bodies, thus saving them from the need to undress or be touched by the male doc-

tor. The little dolls eventually became works of erotic art in their own right, avidly sought by collectors. Here we have a traditionally Chinese doctor's lady: prim, not a hair out of place, a little plump, with slight, soft curves, small breasts, and bound "lotus feet," juxtaposed with a more European version: voluptuous body, flowing tresses, big breasts and hips, and long, slender legs and feet.

FIGURES 98, 99, *and* 100. Reclining Buddha (*above*) (jade, China, eighth century); Hula Girl (*opposite, top*) (ceramic, Japanese export, c. 1950; photo by Adam Stevens); Tongan Beauty (*opposite, bottom*) (c. 1890; photo by Thomas Andrew). Religious art and erotic art, fine art and folk art, and the art of the human form are more closely related than at first appears. Although the male Buddha (fig. 98), painstakingly carved from the most precious jade to fashion the image of a supremely enlightened being; the hula dancer (fig. 99), a cheap mass-produced figurine of pop culture; and the young Tongan lady (fig. 100), a living doll from Polynesia, emerged from very different realms, they can still be identified as "soul mates" because of the attitude they share, one that is natural, at ease, and softly sexual.

THE ARTS OF LOVE

L OVEMAKING IS a fine art. Sex is a natural impulse, but it needs to be refined and directed to a proper end—mutual fulfillment and enrichment of both partners: "In union with a beloved partner, one becomes whole and complete." For good lovemaking there must be ardent passion and an absence of care, worry, and inhibition. In good lovemaking, tension is released, balance is restored, and pleasure is experienced. Clean, healthy, and enjoyable sexual intercourse is a fundamental human right, and the basic rules for lovemaking are universally valid. Two thousand years ago, Ovid summarized those rules in the *Art of Love* (Ars Amatoria):

> Love is a pleasure, not a duty or a mere biological imperative.
> Love should humanize and civilize a person.
> Love is an art that must be learned and cultivated.
> Love depends on the mutual gratification of the man and woman.
> Men and women differ.

In the twentieth century the eccentric psychologist and incurable optimist Wilhelm Reich maintained more radically that orgasmic sex performed en masse could cure just about anything: industrial pollution, infertile deserts, coronary thrombosis, inner-city crime, leukemia. It is undoubtedly true that much of the awful suffering that occurs in this world is caused by those who engage in hasty, domineering, perverse, and violent sex. And "Make love, not war" will always be excellent advice.

I'd like to digress a bit here to discuss a practice common to sexual science in both China and India and not unknown in the West: coitus reservatus, intercourse without male ejaculation. This is the reason there are no "come shots" in traditional Chinese and Indian erotic art (sometimes such scenes occur in modern Chinese and Indian erotic art, but that is because of the tourist trade; Westerners like to see proof of an orgasm). Since a Chinese gentleman had to make love to several women each night, it made sense to restrain himself as much as possible—one rule of thumb was two or three emissions in ten encounters—in order to satisfy all his partners. But the technique became an end in itself and all sorts of wild claims were made: the less frequently a man ejaculated the longer he would live, for example, and by mining the inexhaustible yin essence of one's female partners one could attain immortality. In India, coitus reservatus most probably developed as a means of birth control in Tantric rituals where promiscuous sex occurred, but later semen was equated with enlightenment essence, a substance so precious (it took forty drops of blood to produce one drop of semen) that it should be retained at all cost. If semen happened to be spilled it must be reabsorbed through the urethra with the "fountain pen technique" (*vajroli* mudra). It was believed that if great yogis were scratched, semen, not blood, would ooze out.

The validity of such claims has to be questioned both on medical grounds and by common sense. Among other negative effects, long-term suppression of ejaculation is not good for the health of the prostate. In traditions where no restraints are placed on male ejaculation, people live just as long and suffer no ill effects. In Islamic sex manuals, copious amounts of semen are a requisite for enjoyable lovemaking, and the Muslim shahs of India and elsewhere had ejaculatory sex daily with the women of their harem for years. The twentieth-century sheik Ibn Saud, for instance, is reliably reported to have had sex with at least three different women every night for sixty-three years, a total of more than sixty-five thousand ejaculations in one lifetime. Ibn Saud's secret was simply his delight in the act: "The most blessed thing in life, and the only thing that makes life worth living, is to place your lips on the lips of a woman, to rub your body with the body of a woman, and to place your love organ into the love organ of a woman." In the West we have the example of "Old Parr." After being widowed for the third time when he was one hundred, Thomas Parr was imprisoned for a series of rapes. Parr spent eighteen years in jail, and then he married a forty-five-year-old woman as soon as he was released. He was said to have had sex with his wife nearly every day until he wore her out at age fifty-nine, and it is rumored that he fathered several children out of wedlock during this period. Parr finally passed away in 1635, aged 152.

The unwarranted dread of losing "precious bodily fluids" actually became a social problem in such diverse cultures as Victorian England and Gandhian India. In 1741 a Swiss physician named Tissot published *Onanism, a Treatise on the Disorders of Masturbation*, describing the horrors—insanity, rotting of the brain, premature death—awaiting those who wantonly squandered their vital fluids. This led to a hysterical antimasturbation campaign that plagued Europe and the United States for two centuries. In India the problem was even more extreme. Although Gandhi followed the Tantric practice of sleeping next to young girls to absorb their revitalizing sexual energy, he was fanatically afraid of spilling his seed and constantly fretted over accidental (but natural) emissions. Many middle- and upper-class Indian men shared Gandhi's dread of dissipating precious *bindu* and were loath to fulfill their conjugal duties. Such neglect is contrary to Hindu tradition; a wife had an inalienable right to sexual intercourse with her husband—in ancient India, warriors on the battlefield were granted leave to fulfill this obligation at least once a month. It is more sensible to consider sexual effluvia as an offering to the gods—devout Muslim couples like to cry out "God is great" at the moment of ejaculation—and not be overly concerned with the control or loss of semen.

FIGURE 101. *The Enticement of Ṛṣyaśṛṅga* (watercolor on paper, India, c. 1635; Philadelphia Museum of Art, Stella Kramrisch Collection). Seers, East and West, have taught that sexual congress bestows great benefits to the human race. A severe drought plagued the kingdom of Anga in India, and the king's advisors requested that he seek the assistance of the hermit Ṛṣyaśṛṅga, whose magical powers, acquired through fierce asceticism, were so great that he could summon rain at will. Ṛṣyaśṛṅga had to be enticed from his mountain retreat, however, so the king charged two of his most beautiful courtesans with the task of bringing the hermit back with them. Ṛṣyaśṛṅga, who had been miraculously born of an antelope-mother and raised by a hermit-father, had never seen a woman before, and he was seized by a strange sensation when the

two lovely girls appeared. As shown in figure 101, they pleaded with him to come to their homeland. Unable to resist their enticements, the hermit eventually followed them, and as soon as they arrived in Anga rain began to fall. The king then presented his daughter in marriage to Ṛṣyaśṛnga, and everyone lived happily ever after. (In one version, Ṛṣyaśṛnga and the princess returned to the forest together after the birth of a son, who was adopted by the king.) Celibacy is a valid option, but for a society to truly flourish it needs to have its men and women practicing the arts of love harmoniously and in good faith.

FIGURE 102 (right). *Ascetic Boy after His First Experience of Sex* (red sandstone, India, c. 200–300; Government Museum, Mathura). In a number of Hindu and Buddhist texts, there are tales of hermits like Ṛṣyaśṛnga who had been raised in the jungle unaware of the existence of women. Because of their total innocence, such ascetics are easily seduced when they finally encounter a nubile young lady, and this amusing image captures well the wonder and confusion of a young man (most likely Ṛṣyaśṛnga, who inherited a horn from his antelope-mother) upon his introduction to the arts of love. The bewildered Ṛṣyaśṛnga told his father about his encounter with the strange creature: "The being had black, shiny tresses; eyes like lotus blossoms; a snow white neck; and on its chest were two globes most delightful to touch. Its waist was slender, and its hips round and smooth. The being was as fragrant as the forest flowers, its words as sweet as nectar, and it moved with the grace of a swan. It clasped me in a tight embrace, pressed its lips to mine, making me shudder." Most ascetics willingly abandon their monastic lives to enjoy the pleasures of the body, but many eventually return to the forest after fully exploring the realm of *kāma* (sexual bliss).

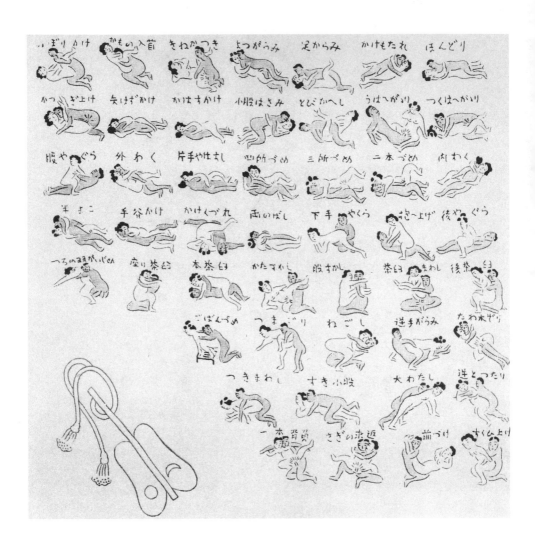

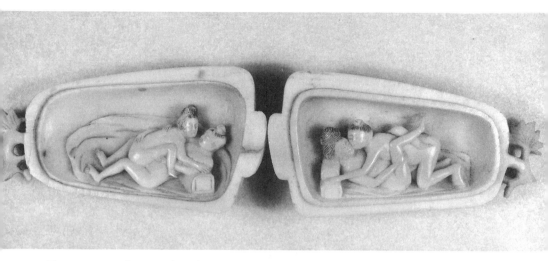

FIGURE 103 (*opposite*). The Forty-eight Postures of Lovemaking (screen-printed silk, Japan, twentieth century). Sex manuals always contain a section on positions for intercourse, ranging from old standbys to the contortionistic. Outlines of the forty-eight postures of love as practiced in Japan are shown here. (Japanese sumo wrestling also has forty-eight basic techniques, hence the referee's fan in the lower left corner.) One tradition has it that these forty-eight positions were developed by a Japanese sex shaman to assist childless couples in conceiving: at least one of them would produce the desired result. Another text states, "Practice these positions with imagination, and it is like having forty-eight different lovers."

FIGURE 104 (*above*). Chinese Lovers Taking Turns Being on Top (ivory, China, nineteenth century). Anthropologists have often remarked that some "primitive" tribes seem to have a much greater practical knowledge of how the human body functions during sexual intercourse than many Western physicians do. This knowledge was acquired from careful and leisurely lovemaking. While theirs is not a primitive culture, the Chinese have thoroughly researched the art of love and have realized the importance of sexual give-and-take, as we see here.

FIGURE 105. *Love in the Four Seasons* (woodblock print, Japan, nineteenth century). This print is inscribed with these appropriate poems:

Autumn

In autumn
winds are gentle,
clouds drift along,
and maple leaves
glow in the sun.

Spring

Mingling together,
like budding willow
branches softly swaying
in the sensuous breeze
of early spring.

Winter

Passion,
buried deep
in the snow,
surfaces intensely
before melting away.

Summer

In summer,
the light of dawn
filters through the trees
bathing lovers, in full flower,
with sweet radiance.

An outline of love in the four seasons from Tantric texts gives this advice:

In spring make love in a beautiful hall decorated with spring flowers and sweet-singing cuckoo birds in cages; clad yourselves in fine and transparent gowns. In summer make love in the moonlight, fresh from a cool bath, smeared with sandalwood paste, and caressed by gentle breezes. In autumn wear your best garments, heat the room with a small stove, and sip newly made wine as you leisurely make love. In winter take a warm bath, bundle yourselves in thick blankets, and slow down the pace.

FIGURE 106. Penis Puppet Theater, by Hishikawa Hironobu (woodblock print, Japan, eighteenth century). Play is an important aspect of lovemaking, and here we see a charming old-time sex aid: a *kokigami*, a paper penis costume. A guidebook to this playful art is available in English (see annotated bibliography).

FIGURE 107. Playful Couple (watercolor, China, twentieth century).
Another sex toy, the swing, used in lovemaking all over the world.

FIGURES 108 *and* 109. Acrobatic Asian Lovers (*above*) (watercolor, India, nineteenth century); Acrobatic European Lovers (*opposite*) (colored print, Austria, c. 1830). Gymnastic lovemaking is common in Asian erotic art

(fig. 108), but examples can also be found in the West, as in this print (fig. 109) by Peter Fendi (1796–1842). Much of this gymnastic lovemaking is in fact completely fanciful—either physically impossible or dangerously reckless.

FIGURES 110 *and* 111. A Sudden Passionate Encounter, French Style (*above*) (print, France, nineteenth century); A Sudden Passionate Encounter, Japanese Style (*opposite*) (painting on silk, Japan, twentieth century). Good lovemaking generally requires careful thought to en-

sure that there is plenty of time for pleasant conversation, fine aphrodisiac food, and much kissing and caressing, but on occasion a sudden, passionate encounter can be a memorable erotic experience.

FIGURE 112. A Satisfied Korean Couple (ink on paper, Korea, nineteenth century). A seemingly simple pleasure, good lovemaking enables each partner to savor the essence of life and discover the source of true creativity.

FIGURE 113. Love Medicine (watercolor, Japan, twentieth century). A Japanese lady applies love medicine to her partner's distressed member. The art and science of aphrodisiacs is an important one for prolonged lovemaking. A number of excellent manuals are available that contain hundreds of recipes and directions for love charms, but all agree that the human imagination is the most potent of all aphrodisiacs and that "without harmony of yin and yang between the man and woman neither medicines nor aphrodisiacs will be of any use."

FIGURES 114 *and* 115. Chinese Couple Copes with Child (*above*) (water-color, China, c. 1900); Western Couple Copes with Child, by Elluin (*opposite*) (engraving, France, 1787). Sex produces children, the "crystal-lization of love." The presence of children presents certain challenges to lovers East (fig. 114) and West (fig. 115), but such obstacles are not insurmountable.

FIGURE 116. The Art of Stealthy Lovemaking (watercolor, Japan, twentieth century). Sex is not something to be ashamed of, and children can be exposed occasionally to their parents' lovemaking without harm, but sometimes mother and father do not want to be disturbed. When a couple has children, the art of stealth becomes an important element in lovemaking.

FIGURE 117. Cultured Sex (watercolor, China, nineteenth century). In this dreamlike scene a Chinese loving couple and their retinue look with favor upon the sexual experimentation of a group of young men and women. Such highly cultured sex can be practiced out in the open, free of shame, guilt, dread, or coercion.

FIGURES 118 *and* 119. Individual Sex Research (*opposite*) (miniature, Tabriz school, Persia, eighteenth century); Paired Sex Research (*above*) (woodblock print, Japan, eighteenth century). Sex research can be conducted individually or with a partner. The annotated bibliography will provide the reader with enough information to sustain years of research.

ANNOTATED BIBLIOGRAPHY

General Surveys

Abramson, Paul R., and Steven D. Pinkerton. *With Pleasure: Thoughts on the Nature of Human Sexuality*. New York: Oxford University Press, 1995. Two professors purport to present a new theory of sexuality; a bit pompous.

Bishop, Clifford. *Sex and Spirit*. New York: Little, Brown & Co., 1996. Thorough and well written, with many good illustrations, mostly in color; an excellent guide. Recommended.

Block, Iwan. *The Sexual Life of Our Time: A Complete Encyclopaedia of the Sexual Sciences in Their Relation to Modern Civilization*. New York: Falstaff Press, 1937.

———. *Strange Sexual Practices in All Races of the World*. New York: Falstaff Press, 1933. Two rambling studies by the famed German sexologist.

Blum, Deborah. *Sex on the Brain: The Biological Differences between Men and Women*. New York: Penguin Books, 1997. Well-written survey of contemporary scientific views of sex and sexuality.

Bowie, Theodore, ed. *Studies in Erotic Art*. New York: Basic Books, 1970. Scholarly illustrated essays on Greco-Roman erotic art, pre-Columbian erotic ceramics, Japanese *shunga*, Michelangelo's *Pieta*, and Picasso's erotic works.

Brash, R. *How Did Sex Begin?* New York: David McKay, 1973. General, rather superficial, survey.

Brend, William A. *Sacrifice to Attis: A Study of Sex and Civilization*. London: Heinemann, 1936. An early study of sex and (Western) civilization; deals largely with the irrational fear of sex in Western culture; for example, the frontispiece depicts the clamp used in castration ceremonies of the priests of Attis.

Burton, E., ed., *Venus Oceanica*. New York: The Oceanica Research Press, 1935. Despite the irritating, condescending, and racist perspectives of the physicians who authored the essays featured here ("The Sexual Life of South Sea Natives," "Erotic Rituals of Australian Aboriginals," and "Ethnopornographia") the book is full of interesting information and photographs that are unobtainable elsewhere.

Burton, Sir Richard. *The Erotic Traveler*. New York: Barnes & Noble, 1993. A collection culled from Burton's vast corpus; the information is factual and impersonal, which is unfortunate, since Burton had sex with countless women (and perhaps men) from an extraordinary variety of cultures. His personal journals, alas, were burned by his wife, Isabel, upon his death.

Cabanes, Augustin. *The Erotikon: Being an Illustrated Treasury of Scientific Marvels of Human Sexuality*. Translated by Robert Meadows. New York: Book Awards, 1966. A collection of bizarre facts and strange tales. Sample section: Polymastia (multiple breasts), ten being the largest number ever documented; one South African woman had six breasts that were all capable of producing milk.

Camphausen, Rufus C. *The Encyclopedia of Sacred Sexuality: From Aphrodisiacs and Ecstacy to Yoni Worship and Zap-lam Yoga*. Rochester Vt.: Inner Traditions, 1991. Fairly useful reference, with illustrations.

Cutner, H. *Sex Worship*. Great Britain: n.p., n.d. Written c. 1930, it gives an interesting account of sexual practices and symbolism within many religious traditions, from those of ancient Egypt through Judaism and Christianity. Contains very objective commentaries for its time, perhaps because Cutner wasn't a cleric or a professor but an artist with a keen interest in both religion and sex.

Daly, K. S. *Sex: An Encyclopedia for the Bewildered*. London: Aurum Press, 1995. Short, tongue-in-cheek, but informative entries.

Danielson, Bengt. *Love in the South Seas*. Honolulu: Mutual Publishing, 1986. Sex in paradise is much like sex everywhere else: sometimes sublime, sometimes mechanical; sometimes elevating, sometimes degrading.

Diamond, Jared. *Why Is Sex Fun? The Evolution of Human Sexuality*. New York: HarperCollins, 1997. A better question would be, Why is sex beautiful? Beauty is an abstract quality scientists have a hard time comprehending.

Diamond, Milton. *Sex Watching*. London: Macdonal & Co., 1984. Popularly written survey of modern sexual culture; many illustrations.

Douglas, Nik. *Spiritual Sex: Secrets of Tantra from the Ice Age to the New Millennium*. New York: Pocket Books, 1997. A comprehensive and nonjudgmental presentation of Tantra, with much new and interesting information on Tantra in the West; numerous illustrations and line drawings. Includes a Tantra database chapter that lists related Web sites on the Internet.

Dulaure, Jacques-Antoine. *The Gods of Generation*. New York: AMS Press, 1975. Reprint of a book first published in French in 1805.

Evola, Julius. *The Metaphysics of Sex*. New York: Inner Traditions, 1983. A trenchant criticism of modern "sexology" and the myth of psychoanalysis.

Feuerstein, Georg. *Sacred Sexuality*. Los Angeles: Jeremy P. Tarcher, 1992. Study of sex from a New Age perspective; rather dull and bereft of illustrations.

Foucault, Michael. *The History of Sexuality*. 3 vols. New York: Vantage Books, 1984–90. Famous modern study by a well-known French philosopher; rambling and difficult to read, however.

Gilbert, Harriet, ed. *Fetishes, Florentine Girdles, and Other Explorations into the Sexual Imagination*. New York: HarperCollins, 1993. A feminist dictionary, with illustrations.

Gilman, Sander L. *Sexuality: An Illustrated History*. New York: John Wiley & Sons, 1989. Scholarly study by a psychiatrist. Contains many rare and unusual illustrations.

Goldberg, B. Z. *The Sacred Fire*. New York: University Books, 1958. One of the best early studies, with illustrations.

Goldenson, Robert, and Kenneth Anderson. *The Wordsworth Dictionary of Sex*. Ware, Hertfordshire, England: Wordsworth Editions, 1994. Comprehensive text with erotic woodcuts marking each section.

Goldstein, Martin. *The Sex Book: A Modern Pictorial Encyclopedia*. New York: Herder & Herder, 1971. Short, simple entries but with many graphic black-and-white photographs by Will McBride.

Gonzales-Crussi, F. *On the Nature of Things Erotic*. New York: Vantage Books, 1989. Ruminations on sex by a professor of pathology.

Goodland, Roger. *A Bibliography of Sex Rites and Customs*. New York: AMS Press, 1974. Reprint of the 1931 edition, so good only for the years prior to that; however, includes works "in all European languages," so contains much information unobtainable elsewhere.

de Gourmont, Remy. *The Natural Philosophy of Love*. New York: Collier Books, 1961. Originally published in 1922, this is one of the first unfortunate (and doomed) attempts to strip "love of all mystical and romantic elements and bring it into line with biology."

Gregerson, Edgar. *Sexual Practices: The Story of Human Sexuality*. New York: Franklin Watts, 1983. A readable, illustrated general survey with line drawings and monochrome photos throughout the text.

Gupta, Bina. *Sexual Archetypes, East and West*. New York: Paragon House, 1987. A collection of semischolarly articles, including one by a Moonie, a member of the Unification Church, notorious for staging huge mass weddings.

Haeberile, Edwin J. *The Sex Atlas*. New York: Continuum, 1983. Useful guide to sex in the modern world.

Hamill, Sam. *The Erotic Spirit: An Anthology of Poems of Sensuality, Love, and Longing*. Boston: Shambhala Publications, 1996. Nice selection but could have used some illustrations.

Henriques, Fernando. *Love in Action: The Sociology of Sex*. New York; E. P. Dutton & Co., 1960. Standard survey with good illustrations.

Hoshii, Iwao. *The World of Sex*. 4 vols. Ashford, Kent, England: Paul Norbury Publications, 1986. Written by a German ex-Jesuit priest who left the order, became a Japanese citizen, and worked as an economist for the Fuji Bank. Each volume has an individual theme: vol. 1, *Sexual Equality*; vol.2, *Sex and Marriage*; vol. 3, *Responsible Parenthood*; and vol.4, *Sex in Ethics and Law*. Thoroughly researched but rather dry reading and no illustrations.

Jakubowski, Maxim, ed. *The Mammoth Book of International Erotica*. New York: Carroll & Graf Publishers, 1996. Contemporary erotic fiction from all over the globe.

Kakar, Sudhir, and John Munder Ross. *Tales of Love, Sex, and Danger*. London: Unwin, 1987. Not bad for a psychoanalytic study of famous love stories.

Knight, Richard Payne, and Thomas Wright. *Sexual Symbolism*. New York: Julian Press, 1957. A single volume containing reprints of the pioneering works *A Discourse on the Worship of Priapus* (1786) by Knight, and Wright's *The Worship of Generative Powers during the Middle Ages of Europe* (1866). A still-valuable reference. Essential reading.

Kuhn, Alvin Boyd. *Sex as Symbol: The Ancient Light in Modern Psychology*. Kila, Mont.: Kessinger Publishing Co., n.d. Old-fashioned, quirky survey likely published in the 1920s. Includes a chapter titled "The Language of the Lingam and Yoni."

Laurent, Emile, and Paul Nagour. *Magica Sexualis*. New York: Falstaff Press, 1934. Strange but interesting study; illustrated with bizarre plates.

Lewisohn, Richard. *A History of Sexual Customs*. London: Longmans, 1956. Classic and still-useful study with illustrations.

Longworth, T. Clifton. *The Gods of Love: The Creative Process in Early Religion*. Westport, Conn.: Associated Booksellers, 1960. A little-known but valuable study of the sex gods and goddesses in the classical world; some interesting illustrations.

Love, Brenda. *Encyclopedia of Unusual Sex Practices*. Fort Lee, N.J.: Barricade Books, 1992. Interesting but rather alarming at times.

Lucka, Emil. *The Evolution of Love*. London: Allen & Unwin, 1922. Early study of sexual love in Europe.

Mace, David, and Vera Mace. *Marriage East and West*. New York: Doubleday, 1960. Somewhat outdated but still useful regarding marriage customs in various cultures.

Main, John. *Religious Chastity*. New York: AMS Press, 1913. Interesting study of sexual restraint, a practice that exists in some form—usually temporary rather than permanent—in nearly every culture.

Mantegazza, Paolo. *The Sexual Relations of Mankind*. New York: Eugenics Publishing Co., 1935. Pioneering study, now largely outdated, but still interesting to read and full of anecdotes of bizarre human behavior: a mention, for example, of two poor souls who were rescued after getting their erectile members stuck, respectively, in the barrel of a rifle and in a water faucet.

Morris, Desmond. *The Human Sexes: A Natural History of Man and Woman*. New York: St. Martin's Press, 1997. An anthropological and sociological approach to human sexual behavior by the author of *The Naked Ape*. Many color photographs.

Parrinder, Geoffrey. *Sex in the World's Religions*. New York: Oxford University Press, 1980. A rather uninspired treatment of a most important subject, and no illustrations.

Ploss, Herman Heinrich, et al. *Femina Libido Sexualis: Compendium of the Psychology, Anthropology, and Anatomy of the Sexual Characteristics of the Woman*. New York: Medical Press, 1965. A very thorough scientific study, filled with many unusual illustrations.

————. *Woman in the Sexual Relation: An Anthropological and Historical Survey*. New York: Medical Press, 1964. Less technical than the preceding volume but still packed with information and illustrations.

Richardson, Nan, and Catherine Chermayeff. *Wild Love*. San Francisco: Chronicle Books, 1994. Color photographs of animals in love.

Singer, Irving. *The Pursuit of Love*. Baltimore: Johns Hopkins University Press, 1994. A philosophy professor from MIT ruminates on the nature of love.

Small, Meredith F. *What's Love Got to Do with It? The Evolution of Human Mating*. New York: Doubleday, 1995. Another study on the "evolution" of sex but more interesting than most.

Smith, Robin. *The Encyclopedia of Sexual Trivia: A Collection of Anecdotes, Facts, and Trivia about the World's Oldest Diversion*. New York: St. Martin's Press, 1990. Not as interesting as it sounds.

Spink, Walter M. *The Axis of Eros*. New York: Penguin Books, 1973. A montage of monochrome illustrations and brief captions.

Stern, Bernhard. *The Scented Garden: Anthropology of Sex Life in the Levant*. New York: American Ethnological Press, 1934. Despite the title, it covers most of the civilized world; although an early study, still quite interesting and graced with dozens of photographs of young nude women of various races.

Stone, Lee Alexander, ed. *The Story of Phallicism*. 2 vols. Chicago: Pascal Covici, 1927. An important and still-useful study.

Tabori, Paul. *A Pictorial History of Love*. London: Spring Books, 1966. Popularly written, well-illustrated treatment of the subject.

Tannhill, Rea. *Sex in History*. London: Sphere Books, 1981. Standard general study by the author of *Food in History*, another of life's primal concerns.

Taylor, Timothy. *The Prehistory of Sex: Four Million Years of Human Sexual Culture*. New York: Bantam Books, 1996. The usual evolutionary bias in interpretation but well written and well illustrated.

de Waal, Frans and Frans Lanting. *Bonobo: The Forgotten Ape*. Berkeley and Los Angeles: University of California Press, 1997. A wonderful illustrated book on the "Apes of Venus," primates who exuberantly utilize sex for play, for friendship, for conflict resolution, as a thank-you gift, and for reproduction. Bonobos are also known as the "make-love-not-war primates," and the egalitarian, peaceful nature of their society contradicts theories that stress the biological inevitability of aggressiveness and warfare. Recommended.

Waldemar, Charles. *The Mystery of Sex*. London: Elek Books, 1958. General study, with numerous nonexplicit illustrations.

Wallace, Robert A. *How They Do It*. New York: William Morrow & Co., 1980. Humorous account of love in the animal realm.

Walters, Mark Jerome. *Courtship in the Animal Kingdom*. New York: Doubleday, 1988. Another study of sex among the animals.

Watts, Alan W. *Nature, Man, and Woman*. New York: Mentor Books, 1958. Well written and enjoyable to read.

Windybank, Susan. *Wild Sex: All You Want to Know about the Birds and the Bees*. Balgowlah, NSW, Australia: Reed Books, 1991. With sections on group sex, sadomasochism, and transvestism, among others, in the animal kingdom.

Young, Lailan. *Love around the World*. London: Hodder and Stoughton, 1985. An entertaining collection of sexual lore gathered from around the world, with a few unusual illustrations.

SEX IN THE EASTERN WORLD

General

Cleugh, James. *A History of Oriental Orgies*. New York: Dell Publishing, 1968. Despite the lurid title, a fairly straightforward account of sexual practices in Africa, Persia, China, Japan, India, and Polynesia.

Craze, Richard. *The Spiritual Traditions of Sex*. New York: Harmony Books, 1996. Brief introduction to Taoist and Tantric sexual practices, adapted for the modern reader.

Douglas, Nik, and Penny Slinger. *Mountain Ecstasy*. New York: A & W Visual Library, 1978. A collection of erotic montages accompanied by quotations and original poems.

———. *The Pillow Book: The Erotic Sentiment and the Paintings of India, Nepal, China, and Japan*. New York: Destiny Books, 1984. Illustrations all in color; the examples from Nepal are outstanding. Recommended.

———. *Sexual Secrets*. New York: Destiny Books, 1979. Indispensable guide to the "alchemy of ecstasy." Hundreds of illustrations and extensive quotations from the classics of Asian erotic literature. Highly recommended.

Faure, Bernard. *The Red Thread: Buddhist Approaches to Sexuality*. Princeton, N.J.: Princeton University Press, 1988. The book begins with a brief mention of sex scandals in modern American Buddhist communities, but thereafter focuses on the sexual arcana of medieval Chinese and Japanese Buddhism. Includes a long chapter on "Buddhist Homosexualities."

Fowkes, Charles. *The Pillow Book*. London: Hamlyn, 1988. Nicely illustrated in color, accompanied by poetic quotations from erotic literature; covers India, China, and Japan.

Klinger, D. M. *Erotische Kunst in China, Japan, Indien, und Arabien*. 3 vols. Nürnberg: DMK-Verlag, 1983. Hundreds of illustrations of erotic art from Asia. Brief introduction in German and English; minimal captions.

Rawson, Philip. *Erotic Art of the East*. New York: G. P. Putnam's Sons, 1968. Both the illustrations and the text are excellent. Recommended.

———. *Oriental Erotic Art*. London: Quartet Books, 1981. A more concise version of the above book with different illustrations.

Scott, George Riley. *Far Eastern Sex Life*. London: Gerald G. Swan, 1943. Sensationalized, racist, and mostly inaccurate account of sex in the Far East. For some peculiar reason, the author includes chapters titled "Torture as Practiced in China," and "Crime and Punishment in Japan," as if those terrors were integrally related to Far Eastern sex life. Interesting to read, though, to see how far we have come.

Stevens, John. *Lust for Enlightenment: Buddhism and Sex*. Boston: Shambhala Publications, 1990. With illustrations. Recommended as the most complete study of the subject.

Chinese Eroticism

Antoine, Denis. *Perfect Union: The Chinese Methods*. New York: Chartwell Books, 1984. Illustrations in color, interspersed with excerpts from Chinese sex manuals.

Beurdeley, Michel. *Chinese Erotic Art*. New York: Chartwell Books, 1969. Illustrations interspersed with excerpts from Chinese erotic classics. Rather similar to Antoine's book, above.

Byron, John. *Portrait of a Chinese Paradise*. London: Quartet Books, 1987. A well-written, well-illustrated survey of the erotica and sexual customs of the Ching period, the last dynasty in China.

Chang, Jolan. *The Tao of Love and Sex: The Ancient Chinese Way to Ecstasy.* New York: E. P. Dutton, 1977.

———. *The Tao of the Loving Couple.* New York: E. P. Dutton, 1983. These two books by Chang provide an accessible and inexpensive introduction to Chinese sexual practices; some illustrations.

Chia, Mantak. *Taoist Secrets of Love: Cultivating Male Sexual Energy.* New York: Aurora Press, 1984.

Chia, Mantak, and Douglas Abram Arava. *The Multi-Orgasmic Man.* New York: HarperCollins, 1996. All three books by Chia are devoted to the shaky premise that ejaculation is bad for men, good for women.

Chia, Mantak, and Maneewan Chia. *Healing Love through the Tao: Cultivating Female Sexual Energy.* Huntington, Calif.: Tao Books, 1986. Both books contain a hodgepodge of information about Oriental sex techniques. The authors' enthusiasm is admirable, but much of the quoted material is generally inaccurate.

Chou, E. *The Dragon and the Phoenix.* Dumfriesshire, Scotland: Tynron Press, 1990. Aimed at the general reader; no illustrations.

Chu, Valentin. *The Yin-Yang Butterfly: Ancient Chinese Sexual Secrets for Western Lovers.* New York: G. P. Putnam's Sons, 1993. A readable, straightforward account; the best introduction to Chinese eroticism.

Cleary, Thomas. *Sex, Health, and Long Life.* Boston: Shambhala Publications, 1994. Translations of five Taoist manuals focusing on the relationship between health and sexuality.

Dikötter, Frank. *Sex, Culture, and Modernity in China.* Honolulu: University of Hawaii Press, 1995. Describes the disjointed sexual identity of modern Chinese cut off from tradition and unable to adopt Western perspectives.

Étiemble. *Yun Yu: An Essay on Eroticism and Love in Ancient China.* Translated by James Hogarth. Geneva: Nagel, 1970. Many good (albeit uncaptioned) illustrations. Text deals mainly with the importance and influence of courtesans in Chinese culture. A few of these beauties captivated emperors so completely that the women, in effect, ruled the empire. Many parents prayed for beautiful daughters who would be chosen to live in the palace, instead of sons who would be drafted into the army and likely killed in combat.

Franzblau, Abraham N. *Erotic Art of China: A Unique Collection of Chinese Prints and Poems Devoted to the Art of Love*. New York: Crown Publishers, 1977. A collection of fifty-three erotic paintings, reproduced in color, from the late nineteenth and early twentieth centuries (the book erroneously ascribes them to the Ming dynasty, but they are in fact much later copies). Each illustration is accompanied by a Chinese poem.

Gichner, Lawrence. *Erotic Aspects of Chinese Culture*. Washington, D.C.: privately printed, 1957. Based on illustrations from Gichner's private collection; although this edition is difficult to obtain, many of the pieces have been widely reproduced in other books on Chinese eroticism.

van Gulik, R. H. *Erotic Color Prints of the Ming Period*. 3 vols. Tokyo: privately published, 1951. An incredible study that reproduces van Gulik's lengthy *handwritten* English and Chinese texts. The original fifty copies were given to university and museum libraries, but reprints are sometimes available at specialist bookstores.

———. *Sexual Life in Ancient China*. Leiden: E. J. Brill, 1974. An extremely erudite, albeit somewhat stuffy—passages the author deems too racy are given in Latin—study of Chinese sex life up to 1644 by the famed Dutch polymath. Now available in an inexpensive hardcover edition. Recommended.

Humana, Charles, and Wang Wu. *The Chinese Way of Love*. Hong Kong: CFW Publications, 1982. A survey of Chinese eroticism, past and present, filled with illustrations and excerpts from erotic classics.

Jackson, Beverly. *Splendid Slippers*. Berkeley: Ten Speed Press, 1997. A full-color study of the tiny shoes Chinese women wore on their bound "lotus feet." The book examines the facts and fiction surrounding this erotic custom.

de Smedt, Marc. *The Chinese Art of Loving*. Geneva: Magna Books, n.d. Many good color illustrations but no captions and a weak text.

———. *Chinese Eroticism*. Geneva: Miller Graphics, 1981. Excerpts from the *Ishimpo*, with illustrations, but not nearly as good as the above volume.

Wang, N. S., and B. L. Wang, trans. *The Fragrant Flower: Classic Chinese Erotica in Art and Poetry*. Buffalo, N.Y.: Prometheus Books, 1990. A reproduction of the charming woodcut illustrations together with translations of the poems in this Chinese erotic classic.

Wile, Douglas. *Art of the Bedchamber: The Chinese Sexual Yoga Classics, Including Women's Solo Meditation Texts*. Albany: State University of New York

Press, 1992. Focuses exclusively on the written record of Taoist sex classics; the translations are careful and extensively annotated. Includes critiques (mostly nit-pickingly negative and pedantic) of many of the books mentioned here. Nevertheless, a good reference work.

Yimen, R. *Dreams of Spring: Erotic Art in China*. Amsterdam: Pepin Press, 1997. A wonderful collection of Chinese erotic art from the Bertholt Collection of Holland, beautifully reproduced in color. Unfortunately, the accompanying text is printed in very small type and is quite difficult to read. Nonetheless, the book is highly recommended for its beautiful, heretofore largely unpublished illustrations.

Chinese Erotic Novels

Egerton, Clement. *The Golden Lotus: A Translation of the Original Chinese "Chin P'ing Mei."* 4 vols. London: Routledge & Kegan Paul, 1972. An expurgated version.

Hana, Patrick, trans. *The Carnal Prayer Mat by Li Yu*. New York: Ballantine Books, 1990. Along with the *Chin P'ing Mei*, this is one of the two best-known Chinese erotic novels. A contemporary translation by a professor of Chinese Literature at Harvard. Pleasant to read, accompanied by helpful notes throughout. Recommended.

Kuhn, Franz, trans. *Jou Pu Tuan: A Seventeenth-Century Erotic Moral Novel by Li Yu*. New York: Grove Press, 1967. One of the most famous Chinese erotic novels (the other being the *Ching P'ing Mei*). This is another version of "The Carnal Prayer Mat," a translation of a translation (Kuhn's text was in flowery, old-fashioned German) but illustrated with quaint erotic drawings.

Roy, David Tod, trans. *The Plum in the Golden Vase (Chin P'ing Mei)*. Vol. 1, *The Gathering*. Princeton, N.J.: Princeton University Press, 1993. Promises to be the ultimate presentation of the Chinese erotic novel. This first volume (of a planned five volumes) is 610 pages packed with information regarding this huge novel—the cast of characters alone runs 56 pages.

Shen Fu. *Six Records of a Floating Life*. Translated by Leonard Pratt and Chiang Su-hui. New York: Penguin Books, 1983. While not especially erotic, the memoirs of Shen Fu are a moving account of the complex nature of married love in China.

Wu Wu Meng. *Houses of Joy*. Paris: Olympia Press, 1958. An abridged version of *Ching P'ing Mei*.

Books by Howard S. Levy

With the exception of *The Tao of Sex* and *The Lotus Lovers*, most of these books by Howard S. Levy are difficult to acquire, but the eccentric scholarship of Dr. Levy's books should be sampled if the reader happens to come across any one of these rare and intriguing works.

Chinese Sex Jokes in Traditional Times. Taipei: Orient Cultural Service, 1974.

Japanese Sex Jokes in Traditional Times. Washington, D.C.: Warm-Soft Village Press, 1973.

Korean Sex Jokes in Traditional Times. Washington, D.C.: Warm-Soft Village Press, 1972.

The Lotus Lovers. Buffalo, N.Y.: Prometheus Books, 1992. This is the latest edition of a book first published under the title *Chinese Footbinding: The Story of a Curious Erotic Custom*.

Oriental Sex Manners. London: New English Library, 1971.

Two Chinese Sex Classics (The Dwelling of Playful Goddesses and Monks and Nuns in a Sea of Sins). Taipei: Orient Cultural Service, 1975.

Warm-Soft Village: Chinese Stories, Sketches, and Essays. Tokyo: privately printed, 1964.

Levy, Howard S., and Akira Ishihara. *The Tao of Sex*. Lower Lake, Calif.: Integral Publishing, 1989. This is the third revised edition, with nice illustrations by Richard Stodart.

Indian Eroticism and Hindu-Buddhist Tantra

Anand, Mulk Raj, and Krishna Nehru Hutheesing. *The Book of Indian Beauty*. Tokyo: Charles E. Tuttle, 1981. An interesting study of the inner and outer aspects of ideal Indian beauty. Krishna Hutheesing was Jawaharlal Nehru's sister and the aunt of Indira Gandhi.

Archer, W. G. *The Hill of Flutes*. Pittsburgh: University of Pittsburgh Press, 1974. An intriguing study of the Santal tribe of eastern India, an indigenous, non-Aryan tribe largely unaffected by either Hindu or Muslim culture, thus representing the India of old. The Santal attitude toward sex was open and free. The Hindu fear of squandering one's "precious bodily fluids" is totally lacking in their culture: "Young couples come together five or six times a night; after children come they do it two or three times a day; up to age forty a couple may have sex two or three times a night; after forty, they still do it at least once a day."

Avalon, Arthur [Sir John Woodroffe]. *Shiva and Shakti*. New York: Dover Publications, 1978. Classical study by the famed British pioneer of Tantric studies in the West. The following two titles are also recommended:

————. *The Serpent Power*. New York: Dover Books, 1974.

————. *Tantra of the Great Liberation*. New York: Dover Books, 1972.

Banerji, S. C. *New Light on Tantra*. Calcutta: Punthi Pustak, 1982. Includes interesting information on Tantric alchemy, medicine, and food.

Bharati, Agehananda. *The Tantric Tradition*. New York: Samuel Weiser, 1965. The most thorough and detailed study of Tantra philosophy available in English.

Bhattacharya, B. *Saivism and the Phallic World*. 2 vols. New Delhi: Munishiram Manoharlal, 1993. A colossal (1,062 pages) study of the subject.

Bhattacharya, Deben, trans. *Love Songs of Vidyâpati*. New York: Grove Press, 1963. Erotic poems describing the lovemaking of Krishna and Radha.

Bhattacharyya, Bhaskar, Nik Douglas, and Penny Slinger. *The Path of the Mystic Lover: Baul Songs of Passion and Ecstasy*. Rochester, Vt.: Destiny Books, 1993. An illuminating and entertaining study of the Bauls of Bengal, Tantric minstrels of sex.

Bhattacharyya, N. N. *History of Indian Erotic Literature*. New Delhi: Munishiram Manoharlal, 1975. Concise, informative survey.

————. *History of the Tantric Religion*. New Delhi: Manohar, 1987. Another scholarly study.

Dallapiccola, Anna L., ed. *Krishna: The Divine Lover*. Lausanne, Switzerland: Edita Lausanne, 1982. The ultimate book on Krishna, filled with wonderful color illustrations.

Dasgupta, S. B. *An Introduction to Tantric Buddhism*. Calcutta: University of Calcutta Press, 1974. Concise survey of the subject.

Devi, Kamala. *The Eastern Way of Love: Tantric Sex and Erotic Mysticism*. New

York: Simon and Schuster, 1977. An illustrated guide (paintings by Peter Schaumann) for the general reader by an anonymous well-connected American woman (she mentions being entertained by a Maharaja in India) who assumed a Sanskrit pen name.

Dimock, Edward C. *The Place of the Hidden Moon*. Chicago: University of Chicago Press, 1986. Deals with the erotic mysticism of the Vaisnava-sahajiyâ cult of Bengal.

Fouce, Paula, and Denise Tomecko. *Shiva*. Bangkok: Tamarind Press, 1990. Contains a chapter titled "His Divine Sexuality" and includes astonishing photographs of Shivaite ascetics performing "penis killing" exercises.

Gatwood, Lynn E. *Devi and the Spouse Goddess: Women, Sexuality, and Marriage in India*. New Delhi: Manohar Publications, 1985. Scholarly, feminist study of the "spouse goddess" ideal in Indian society. No illustrations.

Garrison, Omar. *Tantra: The Yoga of Sex*. New York: Causeway Books, 1964. Early, popularly written presentation to Western readers.

George, Christopher S., trans. *The Candamaharosana Tantra*. New Haven, Conn.: American Oriental Society, 1974. Actual Tantras are hard to come across, and this is a good translation of a typically demanding text.

Guenther, Herbert V. *The Tantric View of Life*. Boulder: Shambhala Publications, 1976. An exposition of Tantric philosophy by a well-known Buddhist scholar.
———, trans. and ed. *The Royal Song of Saraha*. Seattle: University of Washington Press, 1969. An analysis of Saraha's Tantric songs.

Jha, Akhileshwar. *Sexual Designs in Indian Culture*. New Delhi: Vikas Publishing House, 1979. Covers such topics as sex-based medicine, food, and drink; sex in music, dance, and architecture; and sex in modern Indian cinema. No illustrations.

Kakar, Sudhir. *Intimate Relations*. Chicago: University of Chicago Press, 1989. A psychoanalytic study of Indian culture. Contains a revealing chapter titled "Gandhi and Women"; the confident politician was confused and tormented by sex throughout his life.

Kale, Arvind, and Shanta Kale. *Tantra: The Secret Power of Sex*. Bombay: Jaico Publishing House, 1975. Unintentionally humorous treatment of the subject by a well-meaning but misguided Indian couple.

Kvaerne, Per. *An Anthology of Buddhist Tantric Songs*. Bangkok: White Orchid Press, 1986. Extremely detailed, word-for-word analysis of fifty Tantric songs.

Meyer, J. J. *Sexual Life in Ancient India*. New Delhi: Motilal Banarsidass, 1971. Dense, detailed study of the subject by a German scholar.

Miller, Barbara Stoler, trans. *Love Song of the Dark Lord*. New York: Columbia University Press, 1977. A translation of the Gitagovinda, describing the intense love affair between the god Krishna and the cowherd Radha.

O'Flaherty, Wendy Doniger. *Śiva: The Erotic Ascetic*. London: Oxford University Press, 1973. Focuses on the eternal conflict between Kama, the god of love, and Shiva, the god of ascetic passion.

Perera, L. P. N. *Sexuality in Ancient India*. Ceylon: Postgraduate Institute of Pali and Buddhist Studies, 1993. Actually a study of sex in the Buddhist monastic canon, which is, ironically—and revealingly—overwhelmingly concerned with sex and sexual transgressions.

Rai, Ram Kumar. *Encyclopedia of Indian Erotics*. Varanasi, India: Chowkhamba Sanskrit Series, 1983. Useful reference work.

Rosen, Steven J. *Vaisnavi: Women and the Worship of Krishna*. Delhi: Motilal Bararsidass, 1996. Includes several essays on the extremely erotic nature of Krishna worship among Indian female devotees.

Saran, Prem. *Tantra: Hedonism in Indian Culture*. New Delhi: D. K. Printworld, 1994. Brief study with only a few illustrations.

Shah, Pragna R. *Tantra: Its Therapeutic Aspect*. Calcutta: Punthi Pustak,1987. Quirky presentation of applied Tantra.

Shaw, Miranda. *Passionate Enlightenment: Women in Tantric Buddhism*. Princeton, N.J.: Princeton University Press, 1994. Reestablishes women as the central players in Tantra rather than as mere objects to be manipulated by male subjects.

Siegal, Lee, trans. *Fires of Love, Waters of Peace*. Honolulu: University of Hawaii Press, 1983. A valuable introduction to Sanskrit love poetry.

———. *Sacred and Profane Dimensions of Love in Indian Traditions*. Delhi: Oxford University Press, 1978. A study of the Gitagovinda.

Singh, Sarva Daman. *Polyandry in Ancient India*. Delhi: Motilal Banarsidass, 1988. Covers not only India but the rest of the ancient world as well; quotes from Zulu dictionary that defines man "as an animal trained by a woman."

Sinha, S. N., and N. K. Basu. *The History of Marriage and Prostitution*. New Delhi: Khama Publications, 1992. Describes marriage and prostitution in old India and includes an interesting chapter titled "Buddha and the Courtesans."

Snellgrove, D. L., ed. and trans. *The Hevajra Tantra*. 2 vols. London: Oxford University Press, 1959. Another actual Tantra text; volume 1 is the English translation and volume 2 contains the original Sanskrit and Tibetan texts.

Windsor, Edward. *The Hindu Art of Love*. New York: Panurge Press, 1932. Based on the *Kama Sutra* and the *Ananga Ranga*.

Editions of the Kama Sutra and Other Indian Erotic Classics

Anand, Mul Raj, and Lance Dane. *"Kama Sutra" of Vatsyayana*. London: Aspect Publications, 1990. A deluxe edition with many illustrations in color and monochrome. The text is a revised version of the Burton and Arbuthnot translation, below.

Burton, Richard, and F. F. Arbuthnot. *Ananga Ranga*. New York: Medical Press, 1964. This edition contains a few monochrome illustrations and includes the essay "Pharmacopeia: Ars Amoris Indica."

————. *The Illustrated "Kama Sutra."* London: Hamlyn, 1987. Includes excerpts from the *Ananga Ranga* and *Perfumed Garden*. Many illustrations in color.

Comfort, Alex, ed. and trans. *The Illustrated Koka Shastra*. New York: Simon & Schuster, 1997. Comfort's original text (see below) accompanied by many excellent color illustrations. Recommended.

————. *The Koka Shastra*. New York: Stein & Day, 1965. Serious study by the author of the *Joy of Sex* series.

Daniélou, Alain. *The Complete "Kama Sutra."* Rochester, Vt.: Park Street Press, 1994. The first and only complete and unabridged translation. Incidentally, the translator, a French scholar who spent years in India, was an outspoken homosexual.

Krishnanada, Ram. *Classical Hindu Erotology*. Paris: Olympia Press, 1958. A translation of the *Kama Sutra* by a Hindu scholar.

Mannering, Douglas. *The Art of the "Kama Sutra."* New York: Shooting Star Press, 1994. Brief quotations from the Burton and Arbuthnot text accompanied by color illustrations.

Prasad, S. N. *Illustrated Kaiyanamalla's "Ananga Ranga."* Varanasi, India: Chaukhambha Orientalia, 1983. Includes the original Sanskrit text and fifty (rather poor) illustrations.

de Smedt, Marc. *The "Kama Sutra": Erotic Figures in Indian Art*. London: Magna Books, 1993. The text of the *Kama Sutra* accompanied by color illustrations.

Upadhyaya, S. C. *Rati Rahasya of Pandit Kokkoa*. Bombay: D. B. Taraporevala Sons, 1963. Scholarly translation by a Hindu professor, with many monochrome and a few color illustrations.

Vatsyayana. *"Kama Sutra": The Amorous Man and the Sensuous Woman*. New Delhi: Lustre Press, 1995. Two separate volumes bound in one case, with appropriate color illustrations; text based on the Burton and Arbuthnot translation.

Verma, Vinod. *The Kama Sutra for Women*. Tokyo: Kodansha International, 1997. A "reconstruction" by a female practitioner of Ayurvedic medicine, hence there is as much information on health as there is on sex in the book. Also, unlike the original *Kama Sutra*, there are lengthy, and important, chapters such as "Menstruation and Sexuality" and "Pregnancy, Childbirth, and Sexuality."

Khajuraho and Indian-Nepalese Erotic Art

Agrawala, Prithvi K. *Mithuna*. New Delhi: Munishiram Manoharlal, 1983. A well-illustrated study of the "male-female symbol in Indian art and thought."

Ahmad, Maqbool. *Khajuraho: Erotica and Temple Architecture*. New Delhi: Asian Publication Services, 1985. A brief survey with few, badly reproduced illustrations.

Anand, Mulk Raj. *Kama Yoga*. New Delhi: Arnold Publishers, 1991. "Some notes on the philosophical basis of erotic art of India"; many illustrations, some in color, with a section of contemporary Indian erotic art.

Anand, Mulk Raj, and Stella Kamrisch. *Homage to Khajuraho*. Bombay: Marg Publications, 1968. Nice volume on the external beauty of the temples.

Bach, Hilde. *Indian Love Paintings*. Varanasi, India: Lustre Press, 1985. Many fine plates, mostly in color.

Desai, Devangana. *Erotic Sculpture of India: A Socio-Cultural Study*. New Delhi: Tatu McGraw-Hill Publishing, 1975. With monochrome illustrations.

Deva, Krishna. *Khajuraho*. New Delhi: Archaeological Survey of India, 1975.

Deva, Krishna, and B. S. Nayal. *Archaeological Museum Khajuraho.* New Delhi: Archaeological Survey of India, 1977. Two small pamphlets with a few illustrations by an Indian state archaeologist.

Donaldson, Thomas. *Kamadeva's Pleasure Garden: Orrissa.* New Delhi: B. R. Publishing Corp., 1987. An exhaustive study of Kama, the Hindu God of Love. Filled with line drawings and monochrome photographs.

The Flute and the Brush. Exhibition catalog. Newport Beach, Calif.: Newport Harbor Art Museum, 1976. Contains erotic miniatures of Krishna sporting with his lovers.

Fouchet, Max-Pol. *The Erotic Sculpture of India.* London: Allen & Unwin, 1959. Many wonderful illustrations by a renowned French art photographer.

Gichner, Lawrence. *Erotic Aspects of Hindu Sculpture.* Washington, D.C.: privately published, 1949. Pioneering study in the United States. When the book was first published, the author was harassed by postal authorities after he mailed copies to friends, and the book was suppressed for several years.

Lal, Kanwar. *The Cult of Desire: Interpretation of Erotic Sculpture of India.* New York: New York University Books, 1967. Many illustrations.

———. *Kanya and the Yogi.* New Delhi: Naresh Verma, 1970. Explores the nature of asceticism and eroticism in Indian culture, with about fifty illustrations.

Lannoy, Richard, and Harry Baines. *The Eye of Love in the Temple Sculpture of India.* London: Rider, 1976. Nice hand-drawn illustrations.

Lesson, Francis. *Kama Shilpa.* Bombay: D. B. Taraporevala Sons, 1962. An early study of "Indian sculpture depicting love in action"; many monochrome illustrations.

Majupuria, T. C., and I. Majupuria. *Erotic Themes of Nepal.* Lashkar, India: S. Devi, 1990. A detailed, practical guidebook dealing with the erotic art on display in temples in Nepal.

———. *Glories of Khajuraho.* Lashkar, India: M. Gupta, 1990. A similar guidebook to the temples of Khajuraho, filled with much practical information on how to get there, where to stay, good places to shop, and such.

Narain, L. A., with photos by Aditya Arya and D. N. Dube. *Khajuraho: Temples of Ecstasy.* New Delhi: Lustre Press, n.d. Illustrations all in color.

Nath, R. *The Art of Khajuraho.* New Delhi: Abhina Publications, 1980. Detailed, scholarly study with many monochrome illustrations; includes a survey of erotic sculpture throughout India.

Pal, Pratapaditya. *The Sensuous Immortals.* Los Angeles: Los Angeles County Museum of Art, 1978. A wonderful exhibition catalog of the incredibly sexy gods and goddesses of Asia. Recommended.

Poddar, Pramila, and Pramod Kapoor. *Temples of Love: Khajuraho.* New Delhi: Lustre Press, 1992. Excellent color illustrations. Recommended.

Prakash, Vidya. *Khajuraho.* Bombay: D. B. Taraporevala Sons, 1982. A doctoral thesis on the subject published as a book; includes hundreds of line drawings on all aspects of the Khajuraho temples.

Punja, Shobita. *Divine Ecstasy: The Story of Khajuraho.* New Delhi: Penguin Books (India), 1992. A historical study of the significance of Khajuraho in the past and in the present.

————. *Khajuraho.* Hong Kong: Guidebook Co., 1996. Guidebook with good illustrations, all in color.

Rai, Ragu. *Khajuraho.* New Delhi: Time Books International, 1991. A stunning color photo essay by the famed Indian photographer; includes evocative photographs of the modern village of Khajuraho as well as the ancient temples. Accompanied by an interesting essay by the French scholar Louis Frederic. Recommended.

Rawson, Philip. *Erotic Art of India.* New York: Gallery Books, 1983. Forty-eight color plates of erotic paintings.

Reddy, G. V. Bhaskara. *Erotic Sculptures of Ancient India.* New Delhi: Inter-India Publications, 1991. Another thesis produced as a book, but lacking good illustrations.

Thomas, P. *Kama Kalpa: The Hindu Ritual of Love.* Bombay: D. B. Taraporevala Sons, 1960. A classical study of Hindu eroticism, fully illustrated with monochrome photos.

Tucci, Guiseppe. *Rati-Lila.* Geneva: Nagel, 1969. A volume in the Nagel fine art book series that covers the captivating Tantric imagery in the temples of Nepal; beautifully illustrated. Recommended.

Watts, Alan, with photos by Eliot Elisofon. *Erotic Spirituality: The Vision of Konarak.* New York: Collier Books, 1974. Wonderful monochrome illustrations and an elegant text by Watts. Recommended.

Tantric Art

The finest collections of Tantric art are reproduced in the following books by Ajit Mookerjee, each one filled with enthralling illustrations and highly recommended.

Kali: The Feminine Force. Rochester, Vt.: Destiny Books, 1988.
Kundalini. Rochester, Vt.: Destiny Books, 1986.
Tantra Art. New Delhi: Ravi Kumar, 1983.
Tantra Asana. New Delhi: Ravi Kumar, 1971.
Yoga Art. London: Thames & Hudson, 1975.
Mookerjee, Ajit, and Madhu Khanna. *The Tantric Way: Art, Science, Ritual*. Boston: New York Graphic Society, 1977.

Other good books on Tantric art:

Douglas, Nik. *Tantra Yoga*. New Delhi: Munishiram Manoharlal, 1971.
Khanna, Madhu. *Yantra*. London: Thames & Hudson, 1979.
Mandal, Gabriele. *Tantra: Rites of Love*. New York: Rizzoli, 1979. Very brief introduction with forty uncaptioned illustrations in color.
Rawson, Philip. *Tantra: Hayward Galleries Exhibition Catalogue*. London: Arts Council of Great Britain, 1971. Much of the text and many of the illustrations were incorporated into the books listed below; both are highly recommended.

———. *The Art of Tantra*. Rev. ed. New York: Oxford University Press, 1978.
———. *Tantra*. London: Thames & Hudson, 1973.
Sinha, Indra. *The Great Book of Tantra*. Rochester, Vt.: Destiny Books, 1993. A lavish production with lots of color illustrations, but unfortunately most are badly mislabeled; the text is similarly largely inaccurate.

The Sixth Dalai Lama and Tibetan Sexuality

Aris, Michael. *Hidden Treasures and Secret Lives*. New Delhi: Motilal Banarsidass, 1988. The most complete study available in English on the sixth Dalai Lama, the Buddhist lover extraordinaire.

Baker, Ian A. *The Tibetan Art of Healing*. London: Thames & Hudson, 1997. Includes an illustrated section on sex and sexual health.

Barks, Coleman, trans. *Stallion on a Frozen Lake: Love Songs of the Sixth Dalai Lama*. Athens, Ga.: Maypop Books, 1992. Unadorned English versions of the poems; very brief introduction; no commentary.

Campbell, June. *Traveller in Space: In Search of Female Identity in Tibetan Buddhism*. New York: George Braziller, 1996. A serious, scholarly study, most interesting for the revelation that the author was requested to become the secret sexual consort of a high-ranking, ostensibly celibate Tibetan lama; discusses the unpleasant consequences that arose after she went public with the affair.

Chöpel, Gedün. *Tibetan Arts of Love*. Translated and edited by Jeffrey Hopkins. Ithaca, N.Y.: Snow Lion Publications, 1992. A detailed "treatise on passion" by a renegade monk. Heavily annotated, but no illustrations, unfortunately.

Delattre, Pierre. *Tales of a Dalai Lama*. Berkeley: Creative Arts Book Co., 1971. Dreamy fictionalized tales, including one entitled "The Phantom Lover" concerning the sixth Dalai Lama.

Dhondup, K., trans. *Songs of the Sixth Dalai Lama*. Dharmsala, India: Library of Tibetan Works and Archives, 1991. A traditional Tibetan view of the life and songs of the sixth Dalai Lama.

Dorje, Rinjing, trans. *Tales of Uncle Tompa: The Legendary Rascal of Tibet*. San Raphael, Calif.: Dorje Ling, 1975. A loving account of the humorous sexual escapades of Tompa, Tibet's Casanova.

Dowman, Keith. *The Divine Madman*. Clearlake, Calif.: Dawn Horse Press, 1983. The ribald life and erotic Buddhist teachings of Drukpa Kunley, the sex saint of Tibet.

Fields, Rick, and Brian Cutillo, trans. *The Turquoise Bee: The Lovesongs of the Sixth Dalai Lama*. New York: HarperCollins, 1994. The most thoughtfully produced edition of the love songs: originals in calligraphic *ume* script, with poetic English translation, and attractive illustrations by Mayumi Oda.

Houston, G. W., trans. *Wings of the White Crane*. New Delhi: Motilal Banarsidass, 1982. The sixth Dalai Lama's poems translated by an American Christian clergyman and professor.

Maiden, Anne Hubbell, and Edie Farwell. *The Tibetan Art of Parenting: From be-*

fore Conception through Early Childhood. Boston: Wisdom Publications, 1997. Not specifically about sex, but includes chapters on preconception, conception, and gestation.

Sorensen, Per K. *Divinity Secularized: An Inquiry into the Nature and Form of the Songs Ascribed to the Sixth Dalai Lama*. Vienna: Arbeitskreis für Tibetische und Buddhistische Studien Universitat Wien, 1990. A minute, word-for-word analysis of all the songs attributed to the sixth Dalai Lama. One of the commentaries on a song of only six short lines runs more than ten pages.

Tatz, Mark, trans. "Songs of the Sixth Dalai Lama." *The Tibet Journal* 6, no. 4 (winter 1981), 13–31. Yet another version.

Japanese Eroticism

Araki, Nobuyoshi. *Araki: Tokyo Lucky Hole*. Cologne: Benedikt Taschen, 1997. An enormous collection of uncaptioned photographs graphically depicting sex life in Tokyo's sin city. Sordid but revealing, and most of the women are shown smiling gaily.

de Becker, J. E. *Yoshiwara: The Nightless City*. New York: Frederick Publications, 1960. First published in 1899; a bit Victorian in outlook but quite thorough in detail regarding the famed pleasure quarter of old Japan.

Beurdeley, Michel, et al. *Erotic Art of Japan*. Paris: Leon Amiel Publisher, n.d. Illustrations interspersed with excerpts from Japanese erotic classics.

Bornoff, Nicholas. *Pink Samurai*. London: Grafton Books, 1991. A lengthy, enjoyable account of sex in modern Japan. Recommended.

Busch, Heather, and Burton Silver. *Kokigami: The Intimate Art of the Little Paper Costume*. Berkeley: Ten Speed Press, 1990. *Kokigami* are paper penis costumes used in Japan to enhance foreplay (see p. 132); this delightful manual comes complete with cutouts.

Constantine, Peter. *Japan's Sex Trade*. Tokyo: Charles E. Tuttle, 1993. Less comprehensive and more sensational than Bornoff's book, focusing more on Japanese lowlife.

Czaja, Michael. *Gods of Myth and Stone*. Tokyo: Weatherhill, 1974. A well-researched and well-illustrated study of sex in Japanese folk religion.

Evans, Tom, and Mary Anne Evans. *Shunga: The Art of Love in Japan*. New York: Bookthrift, 1975. The most comprehensive survey of the subject in English.

Fagioli, Marco. *Shunga: The Erotic Art of Japan*. New York: Universe Publishing, 1997. Many excellent color illustrations accompanied by an informative text.

Gichner, Lawrence. *Erotic Aspects of Japanese Culture*. Washington, D.C.: privately published, 1953. Descriptions of pieces in Gichner's extensive private collection.

Grosbois, Charles. *Shunga*. Geneva: Nagel Publications, 1964. Part of the Nagel fine art book series on erotic art of the world. Excellent illustrations.

Hidaka, Noboru. *Sex in Japan*. New York: Vantage Press, 1982. Text is peculiar and a bit offensive, but the book reproduces Shozami Koikawa's erotic woodblock prints from *Fifty-three Stations of Tokkaidō* and some other unusual Japanese erotic art in monochrome.

Hokusai, Katsushika. *"The Gifted Venus" by Hokusai*. Translated by Peter Dale. Tokyo: Sei Sei Doh USA, 1980. A reproduction of the original text and woodblock prints plus English translation. Includes a brief introduction to Hokusai's life and art.

Illing, Richard. *Japanese Erotic Art and the Life of the Courtesan*. New York: St. Martin's Press, 1978. Forty color plates with informative commentaries.

Longstreet, Stephen, and Ethel Longstreet. *Yoshiwara: The Pleasure Quarters of Old Tokyo*. Tokyo: Yen Books, 1970. For the general reader.

Mandel, Gabriele. *The Poem of the Pillow*. London: Omega Books, 1984. Many illustrations; weak text and confused layout.

———. *Shunga: Erotic Figures in Japanese Art*. London: Omega Books, 1983. Same comment as above, but illustrations not as good.

Marhenke, Dorit, and May Ekkehard. *Shunga: Erotic Art in Japan*. Heidelberg: Horst Becker, 1995. Many good color illustrations; text in German.

Richie, Donald, and Kenkichi Ito. *The Erotic Gods: Phallicism in Japan*. Tokyo: Zufushinsha, 1967. First-rate text and many excellent and unusual photographs; recommended, but unfortunately extremely difficult to locate.

Seigle, Cecilia Segawa. *Yoshiwara*. Honolulu: University of Hawaii Press, 1993. Scholarly, sympathetic study of the subject by a female university professor.

Soulié, Bernard. *The Japanese Art of Loving*. Translated by Evelyn Rossiter. Geneva: Magna Books, 1993. Lots of color illustrations, unfortunately mostly un- or miscaptioned; very ill-organized text.

Utamaro, Kitagawa. *The Merry Drinkers*. Translated by Peter Dale. Tokyo: Sei Sei Doh USA, 1980. Reproduces the original text and woodblock prints of one of Utamaro's erotic masterpieces; with English translation.

After decades of censorship, unexpurgated *shunga* can now be published in the land of its origin. The series *Ukiyo-E Shunga Meihin Shusei* (Classics of Shunga), published in Tokyo by Kawade Shobō Shinsho over the years 1995–1999, reproduces famous erotic works in large format and in color; each volume also includes an English commentary by Richard Lane. Following are the numbered volumes:

1. *Hokusai En-Musubi Izumono-Sugi* (Hokusai: The Horny God of Izumo)
2. *Utamaro: Ehon Komachi-Biki* (Utamaro: Embracing Venus)
3. *Koryūsai: Shikidō Tokkumi Jūni-Tsugai* (Koryūsai: Twelve Bouts for Eros)
4. *Shigenobu: Yanagi no Arashi* (Shigenobu: Willow Storm)
5. *Eisen: Haru no Usuyuki* (Eisen: Passion in the Snows of Spring)
6. *Kunisada: Koi no Yatsu Fuji* (Kunisada: Love in Eight Directions)
7. *Hokusai: Azuma Nishiki* (Hokusai: Brocade of the East Shunga Album)
8. *Kunisada: Shunshoku Hatsune no Ume* (Kunisada: The Utagawa School and the World of Shunga)
9. *Eiri: Fumi no Kiyogaki* (Eiri: Love Letters, Love Consummated)
10. *Kunisada: Kaidan Yoru no Tono* (Kunisada: Erotic Vignettes)
11. *Masanobu: Neya no Hinagata* (Masanobu: Dyed Patterns of the Boudoir)
12. *Kuniyoshi: Hana-Goyomi* (Kuniyoshi: Love Calendar)
13. *Hokusai: Tsui no Hinagata* (Hokusai: Patterns of Loving Couples)
14. *Eisen: Ehon Hana no Oku* (Eisen: Deep Inside the Flower)
15. *Utamaro: Negai no Itoguchi* (Utamaro: The Prelude to Desire)
16. *Kuniyoshi: Chushingura Kōhen* (Kuniyoshi: The Treasury of the Loyal Retainers)
17. *Koshibagaki-zoshi* (Anonymous: The Brushwood-Fence Scroll)
18. *Utamaro: Ehon Hana Fubuki* (Utamaro: The Joy of Male-Female Coupling)
19. *Kunisada: Shoutsushi Aioi Genji* (Kunisada: True Love Tales of Genji)
20. *Moronobu: Koi no Kiwami* (Moronobu: Climax of Love)
21. *Harunobu: Fūryū Edō Hakkei* (Harunobu: Eight Views of Erotic Edō)
22. *Hokusai: Fukuju So* (Hokusai: Eternal Life)
23. *Sugimura: Kōshoku Hanazakari* (Sugimura: An Abundance of Erotic Love)
24. *Kiyonaga: Sode no Maki* (Kiyonaga: Rolled Sleeves)
25. *Edō no Haru: Inajin Mankai* (Edō Spring: Foreigners in Shunga)

Also recommended is *Makura-e* (Pillow Books), published in two volumes by Gakken (Tokyo, 1995). The illustrations are beautifully reproduced and include captions by Richard Lane.

Sex in the Western World

General

Aries, Philippe, and Andre Bejin, eds. *Western Sexuality*. London: Blackwell, 1985. A collection of scholarly essays on European sexuality.

Basserman, Lugo. *The Oldest Profession: A History of Prostitution*. New York: Dorset Press, 1988. The history of prostitution in Europe, with illustrations.

Bataille, George. *Eroticism, Death, and Sensuality*. San Francisco: City Lights Books, 1986. English translation of a work by a French philosopher; dense, but more accessible and less irritating than the works of Michel Foucault.

Bergman, Martin S. *The Anatomy of Loving*. New York: Fawcett Columbine, 1987. Love through the ages as interpreted by a psychoanalyst.

Bleuel, Hans Peter. *Sex and Society in Nazi Germany*. New York: Dorset Books, 1996. Horrifying reading; the Nazis' perversion of sex was directly related to the commission of other heinous crimes.

Bloch, Ivan. *Sexual Life in England: Past and Present*. London: Oracle Books, 1996. Originally published in 1938. The German scholar Bloch focuses mainly on the darker side of English sexuality: "defloration mania," "flagellation mania," and so on.

Boulware, Jack. *Sex: American Style*. Venice, Calif.: Feral House, 1997. An unabashed and sardonic look at American popular sexual culture, which comes across as being pretty sordid and lewd. The final chapter, "Return to the Flesh District," has a hilarious account of the Good Vibrations twentieth anniversary party. Monochrome illustrations throughout.

Brown, Peter. *The Body and Society*. New York: Columbia University Press, 1988. An extremely thorough (and rather disheartening) study of "men, women, and sexual renunciation" in early Christianity.

Brown, Sanger. *Sex Worship and Symbolism*. Boston: Gorham Press, 1922. Early and now largely outdated study.

Brusendorff, Ove, and Paul Hennington. *The Complete History of Eroticism*. Secaucus, N.J.: Castle, 1965. Huge (one thousand pages) history of eroticism in the West with hundreds of illustrations, unfortunately rather poorly reproduced.

Bryk, Felix. *Voodoo-Eros: Ethnological Studies in the Sex-Life of the African Aborigines*. Translated by Mayne F. Sexton. New York: United Book Guild, 1964. Originally published in 1925. With some illustrations; not nearly as good as *Black Eros* (see de Rachewiltz below).

Bullough, Vern L. *Science in the Bedroom: The History of Sex Research*. New York: Basic Books, 1994. Good reference work; describes the personal character and theories of all the sex researchers of the last 150 years.

Bullough, Vern L., and James Brundage. *Sexual Practices and the Medieval Church*. Buffalo, N.Y.: Prometheus Books, 1982. Covers all aspects, including homosexuality.

Cawthorne, Nigel. *Sex Lives of the Great Dictators*. London: Prion, 1996.

———. *The Sex Lives of the Kings and Queens of England*. London: Prion, 1994.

———. *Sex Lives of the Popes*. London: Prion, 1996.

———. *Sex Lives of the U.S. Presidents*. London: Prion, 1996. All four books alternatingly amusing and appalling.

Cherici, Peter. *Celtic Sexuality*. London: Duckworth, 1994. Well researched and informative, with some illustrations.

Cleugh, James. *Love Locked Out*. London: Spring Books, 1963. A survey of love, license, and restrictions in the Middle Ages.

Cohen, Chapman. *Religion and Sex*. New York: AMS Press, 1919. An early study centering on the pathology of sex and religion.

Crenshaw, Theresa L. *The Alchemy of Love and Lust: How Our Sex Hormones Influence Our Relationships*. New York: Pocket Books, 1996. Blames everything on hormones—including male adultery—but does contain this choice piece of advice: masturbation by women (the more, the better) relieves PMS and can sometimes trigger menstruation.

D'Emillio, John, and Estelle B. Freedman. *Intimate Matters: A History of Sexuality in America*. New York: Harper & Row, 1988. Comprehensive history with sixty-seven illustrations. Curiously, two of the illustrations are execution photographs of three Mexican men and one black man lynched for raping white women (in two separate incidents).

Deveney, John Patrick. *Paschal Beverly Randolf.* Albany, N.Y.: State University of New York Press, 1996. Scholarly work on a black American spiritualist and sex magician. Includes the texts of two works by Randolf on sex magic.

Devereau, Charles. *Venus in India.* Los Angeles: Holloway House Publishing Co., 1967. The erotic adventures of a sex-mad British military man in India; spends his time seducing the daughters of his commander rather than sporting with the native girls.

Fischer, Helen. *Anatomy of Love: A Natural History of Mating, Marriage, and Why We Stray.* New York: Fawcett, 1992. Perhaps the best of the many misguided attempts by scientists to define sex primarily in terms of (socio-) biology and evolution.

Flem, Lydia. *Casanova: The Man Who Really Loved Women.* New York: Farrar, Straus and Giroux, 1997. A very sympathetic study of the famed lover by a French psychoanalyst. She quotes Casanova as saying: "Real love is the love that sometimes arises after sensual pleasure; if it does, it is immortal; the other kind inevitably goes stale, for it lies in mere fantasy."

Forberg, Fred Chas. *De Figuris Veneris: Manual of Classical Erotology.* New York: Medical Press, 1964. Sex in the classical world.

Foster, Lawrence. *Religion and Sexuality: Three American Communal Experiments of the Nineteenth Century.* Oxford: Oxford University Press, 1981. Another study (see Kern, below) of American sexual utopias: the Shakers, the Oneida Community, and the Mormons.

Frantz, David. *Festum Voluptatis: A Study of Renaissance Erotica.* Columbus, Ohio: Ohio State University Press, 1989. The sexy side of the Renaissance, with illustrations.

Gardella, Peter. *Innocent Ecstasy: How Christianity Gave America an Ethic of Sexual Pleasure.* New York: Oxford University Press, 1985. Unlike almost all the other books listed here, this one presents the novel thesis that Christianity was not the sexual poison that nearly killed good sex in the Western world. Not very convincing in light of the ton of evidence presented elsewhere, but interesting to read and well illustrated.

Gay, Peter. *Education of the Senses.* New York: Oxford University Press, 1984. A good study of Victorian sexuality, with some illustrations.

Glynn, Prudence. *Skin to Skin: Eroticism in Dress.* London: Allen & Unwin, 1982. Nice illustrations, including a photograph of the famous *Ecstasy of Saint*

Teresa by sculptor Bernini. This statue of a fully dressed nun is one of the world's most erotic works of art.

Guttman, Allen. *The Erotic in Sports*. New York: Columbia University Press, 1996. First study on the subject; a brief historical introduction followed by a detailed analysis of eroticism in modern athletics and its influence on society.

Haskins, Susan. *Mary Magdalen: Myth and Metaphor*. New York: Riverhead Books, 1993. Informative and well-illustrated study on the "Holy Whore" of the West.

Hopkins, Andrea. *The Book of Courtly Love*. New York: HarperCollins, 1994. Well-presented, illustrated study of the passionate code of the troubadours.

Horner, Tom. *Sex in the Bible*. Rutland, Vt.: Charles E. Tuttle, 1974. Interesting, but not as good as *Sex and the Bible* by Larue (see below).

Iverson, William. *The Pious Pornographers: An Anatomy of American Sex and Other Lively Habits*. New York: William Morrow & Co., 1963.

Kern, Louis J. *An Ordered Love: Sex Roles and Sexuality in Victorian Utopias— the Shakers, the Mormons, and the Oneida Community*. Chapel Hill, N.C.: University of North Carolina Press, 1981. Original, scholarly study of Shaker celibacy, Mormon polygamy, and Oneida pantagamy (group marriage).

Kiefer, Otto. *Sexual Life in Ancient Rome*. London: Abbey Library, 1934. Detailed scholarly study.

Laqueur, Thomas. *Making Sex: Body and Gender from the Greeks to Freud*. Cambridge: Harvard University Press, 1990. Discusses the ever changing views of the body, and the futility of attempting to construct an abstract image of sex.

Larue, Gerald. *Sex and the Bible*. Buffalo, N.Y.: Prometheus Books, 1983. Thorough analysis but rather dull reading.

Lawner, Lynne. *I Modi: The Sixteen Pleasures: An Erotic Album of the Italian Renaissance*. Evanston, Ill.: Northwestern University Press, 1988. An illustrated translation of one of the classics of Western eroticism. Includes the original Italian text.

Legman, G. *The Horn Book Studies in Erotic Folklore and Bibliography*. New York: University Books, 1964. Most comprehensive study of the subject; readable and well researched.

Lewis, Hoag. *American Sex Machines: The Hidden History of Sex and the U.S. Patent Office*. Holbrook, Mass.: Adams Media Corp., 1996. Lively, humorous descriptions of the incredible variety of antisex and pro-sex devices dreamed up by American inventors.

Licht, Hans. *Sexual Life in Ancient Greece*. London: Abbey Library, 1932. Companion volume to Kiefer's *Sexual Life in Ancient Rome* (see above).

Margulis, Lynn, and Dorion Sagan. *Mystery Dance: On the Evolution of Human Sexuality*. New York: Summit Books, 1991. The authors are well aware of the "limitations of biological science," so this book is one of the less-offensive, more-balanced studies of the subject.

Maxwell, Kenneth. *A Sexual Odyssey: From Forbidden Fruit to Cybersex*. New York and London: Plenum Press, 1996. Discusses sex in the modern world and possibilities in the future. The author believes cybersex will eliminate all the nastiness of sex.

Michael, Robert T., et al. *Sex in America: A Definitive Survey*. Boston: Little, Brown & Co., 1994. Perhaps the best of modern American sex surveys, conducted by researchers from the University of Chicago.

Miles, Margaret R. *Carnal Knowing: Female Nakedness and Religious Meaning in the Christian West*. New York: Vantage Books, 1991. Contains an interesting chapter on the nakedness of Adam and Eve; illustrated.

Nicolas, James Perella. *The Kiss: Sacred and Profane*. Berkeley: University of California Press, 1969. Very interesting, scholarly, well-written story of the kiss; illustrations. The best presentation of the subject in English

Odent, Michael. *Water and Sexuality*. New York: Penguin Books, 1990. Deals with the use of water in childbirth and sex therapy.

Osborne, Lawrence. *The Poisoned Embrace: A Brief History of Sexual Pessimism*. New York: Vintage Books, 1993. Depressing.

Ovid. *The Art of Love*. Translated by Henry T. Riley. New York: Stravon, 1949. One of the classics of Western erotica.

Pagels, Elaine. *Adam, Eve, and the Serpent*. New York: Vantage Books, 1988. Takes the Christian fathers to task for, among many other things, making the astonishing argument that every human being is hopelessly contaminated with sin from conception, transmitted by semen.

Panati, Charles. *Sexy Origins and Intimate Things: The Rites and Rituals of Straights, Gays, Bi's, Drags, Trans, Virgins, and Others*. New York: Penguin Putnam, 1998. Pleasant and diverting reading. Illustrated.

Paros, Lawrence. *The Erotic Tongue*. Seattle: Madrona Publishers, 1984. An entertaining and revealing look at "dirty words" in English.

Porter, Roy, and Mikulas Teich. *Sexual Knowledge, Sexual Science*. Cambridge:

Cambridge University Press, 1994. A collection of scholarly essays on the history and development of sexuality in the Western world. Includes an essay on "some traditional views on menstruation and female sexuality" which notes the ascetic Jain view that ejaculation violates the precept of nonviolence: "Each time a man engages in sexual intercourse he causes 900,000 minute beings [sperm] to be destroyed."

Rancier, Lance. *The Sex Chronicles: Strange-but-True Tales from around the World*. Santa Monica, Calif.: General Publishing Group, 1997. Neither as detailed nor as entertaining as *Sexy Origins and Intimate Things* by Panati (see above), and no illustrations.

Ranke-Heinemann, Uta. *Eunuchs for Heaven: The Catholic Church and Sexuality*. London: Andre Deutsch, 1990. A female professor of religion lambastes the Catholic Church for its perverse view of human sexuality, which the author partially blames on non-Christian Stoic, Gnostic, and Manichaean influences.

Riddle, John M. *Contraception and Abortion from the Ancient World to the Renaissance*. Cambridge: Harvard University Press, 1992. Unique, scholarly, and in-depth study of an obscure but important subject in Western history.

Rinzler, Carol Ann. *Why Eve Doesn't Have an Adam's Apple*. New York: Facts on File, 1996. A dictionary of sexual differences between American men and women.

Roberts, Nickie. *Whores in History: Prostitution in Western Society*. London: HarperCollins, 1993. An excellent, challenging, and unrepentant survey of the subject by a stripper turned scholar.

Rusbridger, Alan, with illustrations by Posy Simmonds. *A Concise History of the Sex Manual*. London: Faber & Faber, 1986. An insightful and delightfully humorous look at the sex manual in the West from 1886 to 1986. Recommended.

Sable, Alan, ed. *The Philosophy of Sex*. Savage, Md.: Littlefield Adams, 1991. A collection of essays by professional philosophers; predictably convoluted and dull.

Sardi. *Erotic Love through the Ages*. New York: Dorset Press, 1992. Detailed study of sex customs in the West; no illustrations.

Scheiner, C. J., ed. *The Encyclopedia of Erotic Literature*. 2 vols. New York: Barricade Books, 1996. Selections from the classics of Western erotica from 1527 to 1920 (vol. 1) and from 1920 to the present day (vol. 2). Recommended.

Schultz, Christine, ed. *The Book of Love*. New York: Villard, 1996. Produced by the editors of *The Old Farmers Almanac*, a highly illustrated, popular presentation for modern American readers.

Sellon, Edward. *The Ups and Downs of Life*. Brooklyn: C. J. Scheiner, 1987. Another Victorian erotic classic by a military captain, with some color illustrations.

Singer, Irving. *The Pursuit of Love*. Baltimore: Johns Hopkins University Press, 1994. A professor of philosophy from MIT analyzes sex and love in Western culture.

Smith, Bradley. *The American Way of Sex: An Informal Illustrated History*. New York: Gemini Smith, 1978. General survey with nonexplicit illustrations.

Sprinkle, Annie. *Post-Porn Modernist: My Twenty-five Years as a Multimedia Whore*. San Francisco: Cleis Press, 1998. The totally uninhibited, in-your-face illustrated memoirs of a contemporary sex goddess. A bit alarming but well worth reading.

Steinberg, Leo. *The Sexuality of Christ in Renaissance Art and in Modern Oblivion*. University of Chicago Press, 1996. A truly eye-opening work, both in terms of scholarship and in artworks illustrated. Highly recommended.

Stubbs, Kenneth Ray, ed. *Women of the Light: The New Sacred Prostitute*. Larkspur, Calif.: Secret Garden, 1994. Stimulating essays by a variety of women, delineating the positive aspects of sex work.

Swedenborg, Emanuel. *Love in Marriage*. Translated by David F. Gladish. New York: Swedenborg Foundation, 1992. Sex in heaven as described by the eighteenth-century Swedish scientist-seer.

Wagner, Peter. *Eros Revived*. London: Paladin, 1990. "Erotica of the Enlightenment in England and America."

———. *Lust and Love in the Rococo Period*. Nordlingen, Germany: Dephi, 1986. Many interesting (mostly French) illustrations of erotic art from the Rococo period; text in English and German.

Waldberg, Patrick. *Eros in La Belle Epoque*. New York: Grove Press, 1969. Decadent art nouveau eroticism; many unusual monochrome illustrations.

Wall, O. A. *Sex and Sex Worship*. Saint Louis: C. V. Mosby, 1920. Outdated but filled with quaint illustrations.

Wallace, Irving, et al. *The Secret Sex Lives of Famous People*. New York: Dorset Press, 1993. Entertaining and educational.

Walsh, Anthony, and Grace J. Walsh. *Vive la Différence: A Celebration of the Sexes*. Buffalo, N.Y.: Prometheus Books, 1993. As the title implies, this lighthearted book celebrates—not deplores—the difference between the sexes in the West.

Washington, Peter, ed. *Erotic Poems*. New York: Alfred A. Knopf, 1994. Could use some illustrations to brighten it up.

Weir, Anthony, and James Jerman. *Images of Lust: Sexual Carvings on Medieval Churches*. London: Batsford, 1993. Should be read in conjunction with Steinberg's *Sexuality of Christ* (see above); shows that while not on the same scale as in Hindu temples, erotic sculpture was an important element in medieval church architecture.

Westropp, H. M., and C. S. Wake. *Phallicism in Ancient Worships*. New Delhi: Kumar Brothers, 1970. Reprint of an antiquated text, but contains some interesting old illustrations.

Wilson, Colin. *The Misfits: A Study of Sexual Outsiders*. New York: Carroll & Graf Publishers, 1989. I prefer to emphasize the positive aspects of sex, but this book on the dark side of sex can be worth reading.

Young, Wayland. *Eros Denied: Sex in Western Society*. New York: Grove Press, 1964. Sexual suppression and repression in Western culture, past and present.

Zack, Richard. *History Laid Bare*. New York: HarperCollins, 1995. Popularly written, diverting study of sex in history.

Jewish and Islamic Eroticism

Biale, David. *Eros and the Jews: From Biblical Israel to Contemporary America*. New York: Basic Books, 1992. A historical overview of Jews and sex; very well researched and thought-provoking.

Burton, Sir Richard, trans. *The Perfumed Garden*. Edited and introduced by Charles Fowkes. Rochester, Vt.: Park Street Press, 1989. Abridged (most of the sexist and racist elements in the original translation have been eliminated) and accompanied by color plates of Indian erotica. *The Perfumed Garden* is less pedantic, more bawdy fun than the *Kama Sutra*.

———. *The Perfumed Garden*. Adapted by Jan Hutchinson, et al. New York: HarperCollins, 1996. Portions of Burton's text and additional commentary by Hutchinson et al., adorned with color photographs of an athletic young couple illustrating the described positions in a sunny modern bedroom.

Edwardes, Allen. *Erotica Judaica*. New York: The Julian Press, 1967.

———. *The Jewel in the Lotus*. New York: Julian Press, 1959.

Edwardes, Allen, and R. E. L. Masters. *The Cradle of Erotica*. New York: Julian

Press, 1963. All three of these books by Edwardes focus excessively on the bizarre and perverse aspects of sex in the Middle East (and India); consequently, the books are replete with strange tales and rather unpleasant information. No illustrations.

Hatem, El-Khalidi, trans. *The Fountains of Pleasure*. New York: Dorset Press, 1992. Arabic sex manual. Quotes Muhammad as saying, "One who is able to enjoy copulation and does not do so for any reason is not my follower and has lost the earthly paradise."

Kirsch, Jonathan. *The Harlot by the Side of the Road: Forbidden Tales of the Bible*. New York: Ballentine Books, 1997. Discusses some of the racier and darker tales in the Old Testament such as the "Sacred Incest of Lot and His Daughters" and "God and Gynosadism."

Lamm, Maurice. *The Jewish Way in Love and Marriage*. Middle Village, N.Y.: Jonathan David Publishers, 1980. Addressed to Jewish families but nevertheless useful for researchers of the relationship between sex and religion.

Mandel, Gabriele. *Oriental Erotica*. Translated by Evelyn Rossiter. New York: Crescent Books, 1983. Some unusual illustrations of Islamic erotic art, mostly Persian and Turkish, which is difficult to find. A set of illustrations from a temple in Nepal is mislabeled as being "Indochinese" in origin.

Mernissi, Fatima. *The Veil and the Male Elite: A Feminist Interpretation of Women's Rights in Islam*. Translated by Mary Jo Lakeland. New York: Addison-Wesley Publishing Co., 1987. Includes a fascinating chapter called "The Prophet and Women."

Musallam, B. F. *Sex and Society in Islam: Birth Control before the Nineteenth Century*. Cambridge: Cambridge University Press, 1983. Specialized academic study but useful for those interested in birth control and abortion.

Surieu, Robert. *Sarv-É Naz: An Essay on Love and the Representation of Erotic Themes in Ancient Iran*. Translated by James Hogarth. Geneva: Nagel Publishers, 1967. Many excellent illustrations of rare examples of both ancient and Islamic erotic art; unfortunately, poorly captioned.

Westheimer, Ruth K., and Jonathan Mark. *Heavenly Sex: Sex in the Jewish Tradition*. New York: New York University Press, 1995. Lighthearted, positive presentation of Jewish sexual culture, described as "generous and lusty."

Wilson, Peter Lamborn. *Sacred Drift: Essays on the Margins of Islam*. San Francisco: City Lights Books, 1993.

———. *Scandal: Essays in Islamic Heresy*. Brooklyn: Autonomedia, 1988. Both books include thought-provoking chapters on sex in Islam; for example, "Sexuality and Hermeneutics" and "Eros and Style in *The Interpreter of Desires*."

Winkler, Gershom. *Sacred Secrets: The Sanctity of Sex in Jewish Law and Lore*. Northvale, N. J.: Jason Aronson, 1998. Not as detailed as *Eros and the Jews* but well-written and informative; presents the positive, spiritual aspects of Jewish sexuality.

EROTIC ART COLLECTIONS

World Erotica

The Book of Love Symbols. San Francisco: Chronicle Books, 1995. Little book describing the universal symbols of love and sex.

Bridgeman, Harriet, ed. *Erotic Antiques: Love Is an Antic Thing*. Glenmayne, Scotland: Lyle Publications, 1974. Monochrome illustrations of many unusual erotic works of art—few are true antiques—from various parts of the world.

Brusendorff, Ove, and Paul Hennigson. *Love's Picture Book*. 4 vols. New York: Lyle Stuart, 1969. Hundreds of monochrome photographs, many found nowhere else. Reproduction is rather poor, unfortunately. Interesting text by two Danish sex researchers.

Cawthorne, Nigel. *Secrets of Love: The Erotic Arts through the Ages*. New York: HarperCollins, 1997. Similar in format to the *Erotica* series published by Carroll & Graf but with more Oriental erotic art.

Curtis, Annette. *Erotic Antiques*. Selkirk, United Kingdom: Lyle Publications, 1990. Lots of black-and-white and color photographs of a wide variety of erotic antiques from around the world, many of them amusingly ingenious.

Dening, Sarah. *The Mythology of Sex*. New York: Macmillan, 1996. A Jungian approach to sexual archetypes, East and West, thus heavy on the symbolism; illustrations mostly nonexplicit.

Gerhard, Poul. *The Pillow Book: A History of Naughty Pictures*. Harrow, England: Words and Pictures, 1974. Not much of a text but contains many unusual monochrome illustrations of primarily European erotica.

———. *Pornography or Art?* Harrow, England: Words and Pictures, 1971. Filled with monochrome illustrations but with a poor text—the author fails to make the distinction between erotic art and pornography, and in fact confuses the two categories.

Haught, James A. *The Art of Making Love: An Illustrated Tribute*. Buffalo, N.Y.: Prometheus Books, 1992. Monochrome illustrations, mostly from the West, including some contemporary works.

Hill, Charlotte, and William Wallace. *Erotica: An Illustrated Anthology of Sexual Art and Literature*. 3 vols. New York: Carroll & Graf Publishers, 1992–96. A wonderful series of splendid erotic pictures and excerpts from erotic literature. Highly recommended by my wife Joyce Stevens.

Johns, Catherine. *Erotica: British Museum Pocket Treasury*. London: British Museum, 1997. A little gem of a book with masterpieces of world erotica from the British Museum. Recommended.

Kronhausen, Phyllis, and Eberhard Kronhausen. *The Complete Book of Erotic Art*. New York: Bell Publishing Co., 1978. Originally published in two separate volumes, this edition combines both. Filled with illustrations of erotic art from all over the world; unfortunately, not very well reproduced.

———. *Erotic Art*. New York: Carroll & Graf Publishers, 1993. Contains selected images from the above publication in better reproduction.

———. *Erotic Book Plates*. New York: Bell Publishing Co., 1970. Fascinating collection; a must for all bibliophiles.

Lahr, Jane, and Lena Tabori, eds. *Love: A Celebration in Art and Literature*. New York: Stewart, Tabori & Chang, 1982. Not expressly erotic but full of excellent illustrations.

Mann, A. T., and Jane Lyle. *Sacred Sexuality*. Rockport, Mass.: Element Books, 1995. More of an emphasis on mythological symbolism than on eroticism; explicit illustrations are rather few.

Naomi, Miss. *Forbidden Art: The World of Erotica*. Atglen, Penn.: Schiffer Publishing, 1998. A major collection of erotica amassed by an American grandmother. Almost no text but full of color illustrations of an amazing variety of material published for the first time.

Sacred Symbols, Sacred Sex. London: Thames & Hudson, 1997. Color illustrations of sacred sex symbols with brief accompanying commentaries.

Smith, Bradley. *Erotic Art of the Masters*. New York: Erotic Book Society, n.d. Covers Eastern and Western erotic art in the eighteenth, nineteenth, and twentieth centuries, with reproductions mostly in color.

Webb, Peter. *The Erotic Arts*. London: Secker & Warburg, 1978. Well-illustrated survey of erotic art, East and West, past and present.

Westheimer, Ruth. *The Art of Arousal*. New York: Abbeville Press, 1993. Master-pieces of erotic art, nicely presented in color, drawn from the world's muse-ums, accompanied by commentary by popular sex maven "Dr. Ruth."

Ancient Erotica

Camille, Michael. *The Medieval Art of Love*. New York: Harry N. Abrams, 1998. An excellent survey of the subject, replete with outstanding color plates, some explicit.

Christie's. *Ars Amatoria: The Haddad Family Collection of Ancient Erotic and Amuletic Art*. New York: Christie's, 1998. Excellent catalogue of an extensive collection of ancient erotic art auctioned by Christie's.

Clarke, John R. *Looking at Lovemaking: Constructions of Sexuality in Roman Art, 100 b.c.–a.d. 250*. Berkeley: University of California Press, 1998. Excellent scholarly study with good illustrations in a finely produced book.

Grant, Michael, with photos by Antonia Mulas. *Erotic Art in Pompeii: The Secret Collection of the National Museum of Naples*. London: Octopus Books, 1975. Informative text and wonderful color illustrations with full captions.

Hoyle, Rafael Larco. *Checcan: Essay on Erotic Elements in Peruvian Art*. Geneva: Nagel Publishers, 1965. More than 130 color illustrations, 40 in monochrome, of the astonishing erotic pottery of pre-Columbian Peru: hu-morous, moralizing, religious, and realistic.

Johns, Catherine. *Sex or Symbol? Erotic Images of Greece and Rome*. London: British Museum Publications, 1982. Excellent text and illustrations, some in color; the chapter "Men and Women" has a number of beautiful photographs of Greek and Roman loving couples.

Kampen, Natalie Boymel. *Sexuality in Ancient Art: Near East, Egypt, Greece, and Italy*. New York: Cambridge University Press, 1996. Scholarly essays with about a hundred monochrome illustrations.

Marcadé, Jean. *Eros Kalos: Essay on Erotic Elements in Greek Art*. Geneva: Nagel Publishers, 1962. Companion volume to *Roma Amor*. Greek erotica tends to be a bit more ribald than Roman, with more oral sex portrayed. Looking at some of the statues, the lingering influence of Greek art in erotic temple carving is apparent.

————. *Roma Amor: Essay on Erotic Elements in Etruscan and Roman Art.* Geneva: Nagel Publishers, 1961. Many color and monochrome illustrations, elegant text.

Miles, Christopher, and John Julius Norwich. *Love in the Ancient World.* New York: St. Martin's Press, 1997. General, nicely produced survey of the subject. Many excellent color illustrations.

Mountfield, David. *Greek and Roman Erotica.* New York: Crescent Books, 1982. Not a lot of text but full of color illustrations.

Mulas, Antonia. *Eros in Antiquity.* New York: Erotic Art Book Society, 1978. Many illustrations in color that also appear in Grant's *Erotic Art in Pompeii* (see above), but with only the briefest of introductions and the barest of captions.

de Rachewiltz, Boris. *Black Eros: Sexual Customs of Africa from Prehistory to the Present Day.* London: Allen & Unwin, 1964. Excellent, scholarly study, including a long chapter on Egypt, replete with dozens of stunning photographs. Recommended.

Rawson, Philip, ed. *Primitive Erotic Art.* New York: G. P. Putnam's Sons, 1973. A collection of scholarly essays, with mostly monochrome illustrations, on ancient, Celtic, North American, Central American, South American, African, and Pacific erotic art. Recommended reference work.

Rome, Lucienne et Jesus. *Primitive Eroticism.* London: Omega Books, 1983. Short text, nice color illustrations.

Western Erotica

Adelman, Bob. *Tijuana Bibles: Art and Wit in America's Forbidden Funnies, 1930's–1950's.* New York: Simon & Schuster Editions, 1997. Crude but fun to read.

Aratow, Paul. *One Hundred Years of Erotica: An International Portfolio of Erotic Photography from 1845–1945.* New York: Bell Publishing, 1973. An excellent selection of high-quality old-fashioned erotic photographs.

The Art of Desire. Bloomington, Ind.: Kinsey Institute, 1997. Partial catalog of the Kinsey collection of erotic art. The quality of the exhibited materials is a bit disappointing, but the commentaries are interesting.

Becker, Claus, et al. *Five Hundred Years of Erotic Art*. Hamburg: Museum der erotischen Kunst, 1992. Catalog of the Museum der erotischen Kunst in Germany. Color illustrations of European erotica, entries in German and English.

Bentley, Richard. *Erotic Art*. New York: Gallery Books, 1984. Covers European erotica from "The Classical World" to "The Last Hundred Years." Some illustrations in color.

Bulliet, C. J. *The Courtezan Olympia: An Intimate Survey of Artists and their Mistress-Models*. New York: Covici, Friede, 1930. During the Renaissance many of the models for the Virgin Mary were courtesans. Illustrated.

Di Lauro, Al Rabkin, and Gerald Rabkin. *Dirty Movies: An Illustrated History of the Stag Film (1915–1917)*. New York: Chelsea House, 1976. In the early days of erotic filmmaking, the Americans and the French produced the most movies. American stag films had a more masculine bias; French stag films featured food and drink as well as softer sex.

Edison, L. T. and D. Notkin. *Women en Large: Images of Fat Nudes*. San Francisco: Books in Focus, 1994. A mind-blowing view of a number of American Willendorf goddesses in full glory.

Peter Fendi: Forty Erotic Watercolors. Introduction by William Smith. New York: Arlington House, 1984. The complete set of Fendi's delightful erotic watercolors.

Ferrero, Carlo Scipione. *Eros: An Erotic Journey through the Senses*. New York: Crescent Books, 1988. A well-illustrated guide (in color and monochrome) to sex and the five senses, as appreciated in Europe.

Friedler, Greg. *Naked New York*. New York: W. W. Norton & Co., 1997. Side-by-side photographs of ordinary people in their work clothes and stark naked. Fascinating.

———. *Naked in Los Angeles*. New York: Norton, 1998. Companion volume to *Naked in New York*, with subjects from the opposite coast of the U.S.A. Intriguing.

Hammond, Paul. *French Undressing: Naughty Postcards from 1900 to 1920*. London: Bloomsbury Books, 1976.

Jones, Barbara, and William Ouellette. *Erotic Postcards*. Melbourne: Cassell Australia, 1977. Europeans were really into erotic postcards.

Kahmen, Volker. *Erotic Art Today*. Greenwich, Conn.: New York Graphic Society, 1972. Covers contemporary erotic art in Europe; some color plates.

Klinger, D. M. *Die Menschliche Sexualtät mit Historischen Bilddokumenten* (Human Sexuality with Early Photographic Documents). Vols. 20 and 22. Nürnberg: DMK-Verlag, 1991–92. Brief text in German. Each volume contains hundreds of illustrations.

———. *Erotische Kunst in Europa* (Erotic Art in Europe). Vol. 1 (1500–1880). Nürnberg: DMK-Verlag, 1982. Text in German.

———. *Erotische Kunst in Europa* (Erotic Art in Europe). Vol. 1a (1500–c. 1935). Nürnberg: DMK-Verlag, 1983. Text in German and English.

Levine, Nancy, ed. *Hardcore Crafts*. New York: Ballentine Books, 1976. An illustrated collection of erotic creations by some of America's best crafts people, many of the innovative pieces are a delight to behold.

Lorenzoni, Piero. *English Eroticism*. New York: Crescent Books, 1984. All color illustrations, with many humorous erotic paintings by Thomas Rowlandson.

———. *French Eroticism: The Joy of Life*. New York: Crescent Books, 1984. Full-color illustrations depicting the ardor and inventiveness of French lovers; marred somewhat by the inclusion of illustrations from the depraved works of the Marquis de Sade.

Lucie-Smith, Edward. *Ars Erotica: An Arousing History of Erotic Art*. London: Weidenfeld & Nicolson, 1997.

———. *Sexuality in Western Art*. London: Thames & Hudson, 1991. Two very well illustrated studies, mostly in color, of erotic art in Europe.

Maclean, A. J. *The Secret Art of Tom Poulton*. London: The Erotic Print Society, 1998. An extremely erotic, recently discovered collection of drawings executed between 1945–1960 by the well-known artist and illustrator Tom Poulton. The book also includes two explicit, anonymous novellas written during the same period.

von Meier, Kurt. *The Forbidden Erotica of Thomas Rowlandson, 1756–1827*. Los Angeles: Hogarth Guild, 1970. Presents the work of Rowlandson, England's most notorious erotic artist.

Melville, Robert. *Erotic Art of the West*. New York: G. P. Putnam's Sons, 1973. Covers the subject from "The Act and Varieties of Love" to "The Treatment of Body Parts."

Merkin, Richard, and Bruce McCall. *Velvet Eden: The Richard Merkin Collection of Erotic Photography*. New York: Bell Publishing Co., 1985. Erotic nudes from the period 1900 to 1950.

Nash, Elizabeth. *Plaisirs d'Amour: An Erotic Guide to the Senses*. New York: HarperCollins, 1995. Covers modern European erotic art. In color.

Nazarieff, Serge. *Early Erotic Photography*. Cologne: Benedikt Taschen, 1993. Full of captivating illustrations. Recommended.

Néret, Gilles. *Erotic Art*. Edited by Angelika Muthesius and Burkhard Riemschneider. New York: Taschen, 1998. A revised version of *Twentieth-Century Erotic Art*.

———. *Erotica Universalis*. Cologne: Benedikt Taschen, 1994. Despite the title, the book covers only the Western world, but is an amazing collection of erotica spanning the centuries from antiquity to the present day, with many plates in color. Recommended.

———. *Twentieth-Century Erotic Art*. Cologne: Benedikt Taschen, 1993. Nice illustrations but no truly great pieces.

Paroissien, Leon, and Dinah Dysart, eds. *Eroticism: Images of Sexuality in Australian Art*. Sydney: Fine Arts Press, 1992. Sex down under. Illustrated.

Raffaelli, Ralph. *Rapture: Thirteen Erotic Fantasies*. New York: Grove Press, 1975. Sexy black-and-white photographs of liberated couples acting out their erotic fantasies in uninhibited 1970s fashion.

Rops, Félicien. *The Graphic Work of Félicien Rops*. New York: Land's End Press, 1968. A collection of erotic work by the troubled nineteenth-century Belgian. His art is described as "profound, volcanic, and fearful."

Simpson, Milton. *Folk Erotica: Celebrating Centuries of Erotic Americana*. New York: HarperCollins, 1994. Delightful catalog in full color. Recommended.

Skelton, Christopher. *Eric Gill: The Engravings*. Boston: David R. Godine, 1990. Wonderful, highly erotic art by the famed Roman Catholic engraver and graphic artist. Recommended.

Smith, Bradley. *The American Way of Sex: An Informal Illustrated History*. New York: Gemini Smith, 1978. A well-written, illustrated account of sex in the United States.

———. *Twentieth-Century Masters of Erotic Art*. New York: Fleetbooks, 1980. In color. More encouraging than *Twentieth-Century Erotic Art* by Néret (see above).

Staggers, Rundu. *Body and Soul: Black Erotica by Rundu*. New York: Crown Publishers, 1996. Excellent photography; highly sensual images.

Tilly, Andrew. *Erotic Drawings*. Oxford: Phadon Press, 1986. Classical erotic drawings, in color.

Vargas, Ava. *La Casa de Cita: Mexican Photographs from the Belle Epoque*. London: Quartet Books, 1986. Charming, highly erotic nudes from Mexico. The photographs were discovered in a flea market in 1975.

Weiermair, Peter, ed. *Erotic Art: From the Seventeenth to the Twentieth Century*. Frankfurt: Frankfurter Kunstverein, 1995. Covers European erotic art. In color.

Zichy, Mihály. *The Erotic Drawings of Mihály Zichy*. New York: Grove Press, 1969. A collection of sketches by one of Europe's major erotic artists.

SEX MANUALS

Aldred, Caroline. *Divine Sex: The Tantric and Taoist Arts of Conscious Loving*. New York: HarperCollins, 1996. Oriental sex techniques presented to the Western reader in an easy-to-digest format; excellent, enticing illustrations.

Botting, Kate, and Douglas Botting. *Sex Appeal: The Art and Science of Sexual Attraction*. New York: St. Martin's Press, 1995. Deals with the external trappings of sex appeal but concedes that the brain is the most important element in sexual attraction.

Chia, Mantak, and Douglas Abrams Arava. *The Multi-Orgasmic Man: Sexual Secrets Every Man Should Know*. New York: HarperCollins, 1996. The secret? Don't ejaculate.

Comfort, Alex. *The Joy of Sex: A Gourmet Guide to Lovemaking*. New York: Simon & Schuster, 1972. The popular best-selling guide.

Haeberle, Erwin J. *The Sex Atlas*. New York: Seabury Press, 1978. A massive textbooklike tome with rather dull monochrome illustrations.

Holroyd, Stuart, and Susan Holroyd. *The Complete Book of Sexual Love*. London: Bloomsbury Books, 1979. A reserved, conservative approach to love; very nice color illustrations.

Joannides, Paul. *The Guide to Getting It On! A New and Mostly Wonderful Book about Sex for Adults of All Ages*. West Hollywood, Calif.: Goofy Foot Press, 1997. A hip, streetwise, and good-natured approach to sex; useful for young people. Rather crudely drawn illustrations.

A Lover's Alphabet: A Collection of Aphrodisiac Recipes, Magic Formulae, Lovemaking Secrets, and Erotic Miscellany from East and West. New York: HarperCollins, 1991. Part of the Pillow Book series, a small volume with color illustrations.

Massey, Doreen, ed. *The Lover's Guide Encyclopedia: The Definitive Guide to Sex and You*. New York: Thunder's Mouth Press, 1996. Not definitive—the sex-and-culture section is woefully superficial—but filled with graphic color illustrations, including the details of sex-change operations.

McBride, Will, and Helga Fleischhauer-Hardt. *Show Me! A Picture Book of Sex for Children and Parents*. New York: St. Martin's Press, 1974. Controversial sex manual for children; stark, explicit monochrome photographs throughout.

Quillam, Susan. *Every Woman's Guide to Sexual Fulfillment: An Illustrated Lifetime Guide to Your Sexuality and Sensuality*. New York: Simon & Schuster, 1997. Straightforward and sympathetic guide to fulfilling heterosexual sex.

Winks, Cathy, and Anne Semans. *The New Good Vibrations Guide to Sex*. 2nd ed. San Francisco: Cleis Press, 1997. The most informative general guide available, covering all aspects of sex, with extensive and useful resources and bibliography sections. Recommended; only a few line drawing illustrations, however, so it should be augmented by one of the full-color guides mentioned above.

Lingams, Yonis, Breasts, and Bottoms

Lingams

Anonymous. *Nature Worship: An Account of Phallic Faiths and Practices Ancient and Modern, Including "The Adoration of the Male and Female Powers in Various Nations" and "The Sacta Puja of Indian Gnosticism."* Kila, Mont.: Kessinger Publishing Co., n.d. A reprint of a nineteenth-century work on phallicism; quaint.

Daniélou, Alain. *The Phallus: Sacred Symbol of Male Creative Power*. Rochester, Vt.: Inner Traditions, 1993. A provocative study by the celebrated French scholar; filled with many outstanding illustrations. Recommended.

Jennings, Hargrave. *Phallicism: Celestial and Terrestrial; Heathen and Christian and Its Connection with the Gnostics and Its Foundation in Buddhism*. Kila, Mont.: Kessinger Publishing Co., n.d. Another reprint of an early study of phallicism; similarly quaint, but rather more detailed than *Nature Worship* (see Anonymous, above).

Parsons, Alexandra. *Facts and Phalluses: A Collection of Bizarre and Intriguing Truths, Legends, and Measurements*. New York: St. Martin's Press, 1990. A little collection of mildly interesting odds and ends.

Rocco, Sha. *The Masculine Cross and Ancient Sex Worship*. Kila, Mont.: Kessinger Publishing Co., n.d. First published in 1874, this reprint has some illustrations; quirky but interesting—the author equates "Christna" (Krishna) with Christ and has a section titled "The Phallus in California."

Schwartz, Kit. *The Male Member: Being a Compendium of Facts, Figures, Foibles, and Anecdotes*. New York: St. Martin's Press, 1985. Like Parsons' *Facts and Phalluses*, above, this book has Michelangelo's *David* on the cover, but the text is much longer and more interesting.

Thorn, Mark. *Taboo No More: The Phallus in Fact, Fantasy, and Fiction*. Foreword by Ashley Montagu. New York: Shapolsky Publishers, 1990. States the unconvincing case for the "swaggering penis" as the dominant force in all societies; not surprisingly, it completely ignores Tantra and the creative, all-encompassing power of Mother Shakti.

Yonis

Blank, Joani, ed. *Femalia*. San Francisco: Down There Press, 1993. A little gem of a book: thirty-two beautiful and intriguing full-color close-ups of yonis belonging to women of diverse ages and races. An underground best-seller; would a collection of thirty-two photos of lingams sell nearly as well? Recommended.

Bolon, Carol Radcliffe. *Forms of the Goddess Lajja Gauri in Indian Art*. University Park, Pa.: Pennsylvania State University Press, 1992. Scholarly study that includes many fine illustrations of the open-yoni goddess of India.

Camphausen, Rufus C. *The Yoni: Sacred Symbol of Female Creative Power*. Rochester, Vt.: Inner Traditions, 1996. Companion volume to Daniélou's *The Phallus*; contains some incredible photographs of yonis found in nature, including a stunning image on the cover. Recommended.

Chicago, Judy. *The Dinner Party*. New York: Viking, 1996. A fascinating account of the creation of Judy Chicago's multimedia exhibit honoring the achievements of women throughout history as well as the varied manifestations of the yoni goddess. Its first showing in the late 1970s shocked the art world with its explicit and beautiful renderings of yonis. Many illustrations, some in color.

Dodson, Betty. *Sex for One: The Joy of Self Loving*. New York: Crown Publishers, 1996. Although the solitary thrust of Dodson's work does not mesh exactly with the harmonious mingling of the sexes in *The Cosmic Embrace,* her book expresses the importance, power, and attractiveness of the *yoni* and its expanding role within the context of contemporary American society. The book includes some nice erotic art—the drawings of *yoni* are striking—by the author.

Ensler, Eve. *The Vagina Monologues.* New York: Villard, 1998. An adaptation of the award-winning one-woman show by poet and activist Ensler. A provocative and original approach to understanding the yoni.

Lubell, Winifred Milius. *The Metamorphosis of Baubo: Myths of Woman's Sexual Energy.* Nashville: Vanderbilt University Press, 1994. Detailed study of the ubiquitous open-yoni image; illustrated with many drawings by the author.

Schwarz, Kit. *The Female Member: Being a Compendium of Facts, Figures, Foibles, and Anecdotes about the Loving Organ.* New York: St. Martin's Press, 1988. Companion volume to Schwarz's *The Male Member*; both volumes are rather rambling and a bit flippant.

Breasts

Levy, Mervin. *The Moons of Paradise: Reflections on the Breast in Art.* London: Arthur Barker, 1962. The breast, East and West.

Wilson, Robert Anton. *The Book of the Breast.* Chicago: Playboy Press, 1974. More of an idiosyncratic, disjointed view of sex in general than a study of the breast.

Yalom, Marilyn. *A History of the Breast.* New York: Alfred A. Knopf, 1997. The best of the bunch; extremely well written, with many illustrations.

Bottoms

Hamilton, China. *A View from Behind.* London: Erotic Print Society, 1997. A collection of very erotic photos, including a few suggestive of "the English vice," flagellation with riding crop or switch.

Maitland, Oliver. *The Illustrated Book of Bottoms.* London: Erotic Print Society, 1996. Another publication from the EPS with interesting illustrations and entertaining text.

APHRODISIACS

Most of the erotic classics of the East contain recipes for aphrodisiacs and instructions in casting love spells; the books below are wholly devoted to the subject.

Allardice, Pamela. *Aphrodisiacs and Love Magic*. New York: Avery Publishing, 1989.

Aphrodisiacs: An Encyclopedia of Erotic Wisdom. London: Hamlyn Publishing Group, 1990.

Buckland, Raymond. *Secrets of Gypsy Love Magick: Love Spells, Potions, Amulets, and Charms*. Saint Paul, Minn.: Llewellyn Publications, 1994.

Davenport, John. *Aphrodisiacs and Love Stimulants*. New York: Lyle Stuart, 1966.

Dodd, W. Craig. *A Cornucopia of Aphrodisiacs: Elixirs and Recipes for Love; Nectars and Potent Potions; Sensual Spices; Etc*. London: New Holland Publishers, 1996.

Gifford, Edward S. *The Charms of Love*. London: Faber & Faber, 1962.

Lee, Vera. *Secrets of Venus: A Lovers Guide to Charms, Potions, and Aphrodisiacs*. Bluebell, Pa.: Mt. Ivy Press, 1996.

Rätsch, Christian. *Plants of Love: The History of Aphrodisiacs and a Guide to Their Identification and Use*. Berkeley: Ten Speed Press, 1997. The best of the lot; thorough, with excellent full-color illustrations.

de Roche, Max. *The Foods of Love: Containing the Delights, Vertues, Magickal Properties, and Secret Recipes for All Manner of Exquisite Love Potions and Proven Aphrodisiacs*. New York: Little, Brown & Co., 1990.

Walker, Morton, and Joan Morton. *Sexual Nutrition*. New York: Kensington Publishing Group, 1983.

Walton, Alan Hull. *Aphrodisiacs: From Legend to Prescription*. Westport, Conn.: Associated Booksellers, 1958.